AA

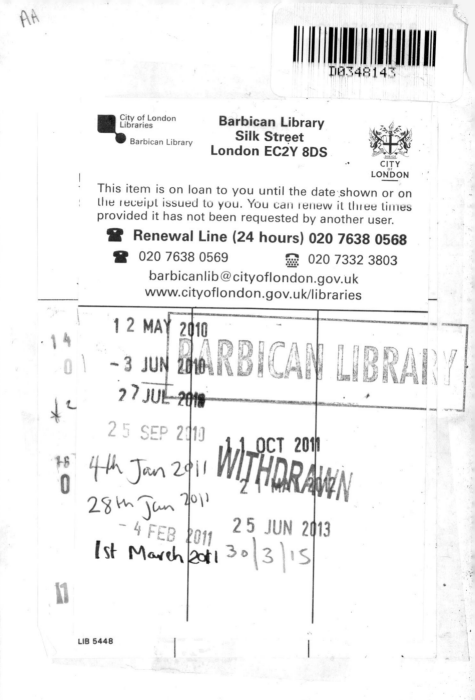

Strindberg

THE PLAYS: VOLUME ONE
THE FATHER MISS JULIE
THE COMRADES CREDITORS

translated by

Gregory Motton

OBERON BOOKS
LONDON

First published in 2000 by Oberon Books Ltd.
(incorporating Absolute Classics)
521 Caledonian Road, London N7 9RH
Tel: 020 7607 3637 / Fax: 020 7607 3629
e-mail: oberon.books@btinternet.com

ISBN: 1 84002 062 8 ✓

Cover illustration by Andrzej Klimowski

Cover typography by Jeff Willis

Printed in Great Britain by Antony Rowe Ltd, Reading.

Contents

Translator's Introduction

Gregory Motton

The fashion at the moment is for versions, or neo-translations, where the aim is to make the text sound as contemporary, and as English, as possible. It is no accident perhaps that this comes at a time of particular homogeneity in contemporary writing itself. We don't perhaps want to hear anything different from what we are used to, and we are used to a narrowing field of variety. How we interpret something seems to be of more interest to us than what the thing actually is. There have probably never been so many different versions of foreign plays going around. It would be a peculiar coincidence however if all the plays ever written from Aeschylus onwards were written in the style of a second-rate British writer from the 1990s. If we ever want to hear anything but our own chatter we shall have to go back to proper translation.

While I do not want to contribute to what I fear is a strong modern tendency to deconstruct even the possibility of accuracy in translation of plays, I would like to make the usual disclaimers of my own translations, emphasising the necessary imperfections of such work and offering it with the appropriate modesty and apologies for any errors, which of course I do.

I should also warn that this is of course only Strindberg rendered into English one hundred years after it was written, and can only hope to give the audience a flavour of the original. Also that the language I use is a hybrid: modern English written in a style intended where possible to resemble the language of another era and another country. I have not used Edwardian English for example, since that in itself would not have reflected turn-of-the-century Swedish very well. Indeed I have tried to avoid idiomatic English altogether, by which I mean ready made phrases, where possible. This is because I think it gives the wrong feel.

(There are possibly those that think this would necessarily result in a colourless kind of language, but readers can judge for themselves. Even when writing my own plays there is a certain kind of idiomatic language that I avoid for its blandness.) Instead I have tried to favour aspects of our English that already are similar to Swedish, using vocabulary of Germanic or Viking origin, instead of Latin or French origin words. Translators into English have the good fortune of being able to chose between three rather distinct layers. It is quite remarkable how often it is possible to use almost exactly the same formulations and vocabulary as the Swedish. The result is a rendition of the directness and simplicity of that language, even when there is a formality in the tone. The Germanic layers of English have the same qualities of expression. It is very convenient.

Where there are idioms in the original I generally try to keep them; that is, I avoid replacing them with a corresponding English one, if I can, unless it is very similar. This is because idioms contain cultural messages and character, and it would be rather contrary to the intention to give a particularly English feel to a phrase just at the very point where it has a particularly Swedish feel in the original.

I think it is the job of the translator to give the audience access to the text, not to put himself and his own interpretation there as an obstacle. As a reader I always feel irritated when a translator has presumed me incapable of being interested in or understanding anything that isn't familiar or even banal. When he can't restrict himself to translating the language, but is compelled to explain the text, or even make it palatable. This same attitude is taken by theatre managements when they look for translations. The National Theatre isn't embarrassed to serve the audience second-rate popularisations of foreign classics where the original is entirely lost; indeed there is no intention to keep it. Perhaps the public gets what it deserves. It is the kind of narrow-minded insular Philistinism which we are descending into at present and which we would be ashamed of if we only had sufficient self-consciousness to notice the pitying eyes of our neighbours upon us.

The customary praise words for translations are 'vigorous', 'startling', 'radical', etc or even simply 'new'. None of these are necessarily qualities one should look for in a translation. In the current climate the real shocker would be 'accurate'. This would be shocking because it would sound like 'dull' (the worst crime), but in reality 'dull' would of course depend on whether the original were dull. It is perhaps indicative of the age that the idea of rendering the voice of the author is not at all exciting to theatre managements. While the marketing departments of theatres are apparently aware of the concept of 'a distinctive voice', this has not led them to expect that any great writer might have a 'distinctive voice'. Instead, theatres and critics talk as if there is a kind of modern stage-speak which, if achieved by a translator, will produce a vital, lively dialogue, and the opposite of 'dull', and that any text rendered into this stage-speak will benefit from its exciting qualities. Well, they are right, in that there is a ubiquitous kind of dialogue and it is a great favourite with second-rate writers and translators alike. Among the latter it is the (new) academic style, in that it is used because approved, and applied as a standard in accordance with distinct rules. Unfortunately, what people think of generally when they hear the word academic in connection with a translation (always used disparagingly), is a too strict adherence to the original; literal accuracy at the expense of spirit. In fact this style of translation hardly exists. Those who might have committed these errors in the past now adopt the current 'Translatorese'; a jollied up, chatty rather loose rendition of the text into (often ill-chosen) idioms.

It is a fitting irony that these are the same types who despise or fear 'datedness', and who always talk of the importance of renewing translations every five years, little realising that it is exactly their favoured style of translation i.e. 'up to date', that dates so quickly. They make it specific to a time (the wrong time) and specific to a place (the wrong place, England).

The generally accepted notion that translations need constant renewing is to some extent absurd, considering that a piece is written at one particular time and is not renewed. So the original will 'date' in that it belongs to some extent to a particular place and time. We may say that anything may 'date' more or less, but just how much and in what way will depend on its quality. Shakespeare doesn't really date very much although his language is old-fashioned. John Buchan however can be said to date. Anything, a work or a translation, will date in direct ratio to its tendency to express itself in terms which lack genuine expressive power but which are instead current and familiar. This is why fashionable things date quicker than unfashionable ones. The datedness of a translation depends partly on the datedness of the original; that is, the way it is interesting or expressive only at the time of its making. A good translation of a poor work will date at the same rate as the original. A bad translation of a good work will date quicker than the original.

Another reason for the 'dating' phenomenon is the idea that a translation should help a work to seem 'relevant'. This is supposed to be achieved by sweeping away traces in the language of attitudes that are out of keeping with our own, and by emphasising that which is familiar. In short, a good translation is supposed to be one which makes it seem as if the play were written in England, today. But this gives a distortion not a translation. Some are willing to have the distortion instead. But they should beware because what is universal and true can be quite at odds with what is contemporary and fashionable.

It is perhaps a measure of the narrow-mindedness of a culture that it feels itself incapable of understanding something from an alien time or place, and instead converts everything into recognisable terms. The result is of course to reinforce its own values and to learn nothing. We fall deeper into our folly, and brook no contradiction. We still perhaps feel uncomfortable with the way Hollywood remakes European films, distorting them beyond recognition to make them palatable to the isolated Midwest rednecks, but unfortunately our theatre is of a similar stamp, to the degree where we think we are making *Titus Andronicus* more interesting by claiming that it resembles Tarantino. Watching European classics in Britain is often like reading the Victorians' moralised versions of Aesop's fables.

In recent years theatres have developed the habit of commissioning 'versions' of great foreign plays. We cannot understand anything unless it is native or has the appearance of being so. We can hear Strindberg if he sounds like John Osborne, or if we can place him in a category and make him a good friend to us and all we stand for. Theatres are preoccupied with being 'relevant' and we have a ludicrously narrow view of what this is, and in fact it is now beginning to mean nothing more than familiar. We think we are iconoclasts but really we seek constant confirmations of our current values.

In short we are Philistines, blind and bigoted. We are not only insular geographically but temporally. Today is more significant to us than yesterday, like children we presume the present is the best of all possible times, and we see the future as the product of our temporary present and are quite inexplicably pleased with that. Theatres regularly announce their 'new version' of this or that classic foreign play, on the presumption that having been executed today it is better and more 'relevant' than an already existing translation – the question of merit doesn't come into it. It is hard to see this kind of fetish with renewal as anything but the result of consumerism's brainwashing.

The ubiquitous chatter and babble that is contemporary stage-speak is the real dullness in theatre, and the addiction to it is an impediment to good translation. For if there is a preconceived idea of what good dialogue should sound like, this will prevent anything else from being heard. Contemporary writers will either imitate it or be excluded, and audiences will find all foreign writers, old and new, rendered into it. Increasingly actors will find it impossible to speak other kinds of dialogue. 'I can't say that, it's not natural' they say (or the director says it for them to justify liberties being taken with a text, by a room full of self-styled experts). But as Beckett replied 'You say it every day'. What they all mean of course is that no one says it on television/the stage etc. But when an actor forces himself to stick to the apparently awkward line of a good writer, the sense of it will reveal itself to him, and will be rewarding.

Naturally with a translation, the actor faced with difficult dialogue has to wonder if the source of it is the original text or some quirk or inexpertise on the part of the translator, and it is largely a matter of trust, unless he cares to check with the original, not in itself a bad idea, and I recommend it. What I do advise is that actors, and directors, should avoid having their expectations lowered by the general idea of 'naturalness' in dialogue, and remember that it is a passing prejudice, promoted by those with a vested interest in mediocrity, and to bear in mind that a great writer is likely to have a distinctive voice. Otherwise how would it be that we can recognise a page of Wycherley, Wilde, O'Neil or Ayckbourn at first sight. No one would say Pinter's dialogue was unnatural. Good writing, like good music, can sometimes be difficult to perform but no one would insist that symphonies should sound like muzak. I have always found that the more experienced or talented an actor is the more he will doggedly bend himself to the line until its logic reveals itself to him – rather than trying to bend the line.

Other translations

Michael Meyer* has translated nearly all of Strindberg's and Ibsen's plays, and it is through these that most of us, myself included, first encountered these playwrights, and we should be grateful that his translations are generally of a good standard of accuracy, that he is good at finding the right word and doesn't make many mistakes. His weakness is the tone. Meyer shares the generalised notion of what dialogue should sound like, and so translates Strindberg into 'Translatorese'. It is the same language he uses for Ibsen, a very different writer. The style is a bit too much that of the English drawing room piece, and as such it carries some of the English class system along with it, which is not of course the same as the

---

* This introduction was written shortly before the sad death of
  Michael Meyer.

Swedish one. The voice is one of easy-going fluency rather than Strindberg's rather less comfortable form of loquatiousness, stilted and passionate at the same time.

Meyer uses English idioms liberally. He makes little attempt to retain the Nordic flavour of the language and uses French origin words where he might use Germanic words. He sometimes uses metaphors where the original is plain, and he extends lines to 'explain' them when he feels they are obscure or difficult. He also has the unfortunate habit of intervening just when Strindberg is most characteristic. When a character looks at a woman 'underneath her eyelids to see what she's like behind them' he gives us 'squinting at her to see what you're like behind that pretty face'. The last three words of that sentence being impossibly glib for Strindberg, and having a very English feel to them. When you translate it back into Swedish, it sounds, in a Swedish context, as if the character is insane, or at least horribly inane. Meyer uses the expression because he judged that eyelids was a synecdoche for beauty, and so wanted to indicate this. His mistake, in my opinion, is that he ends up explaining the line unnecessarily, and inadvertently alters the whole tone of it in doing so. Leaving eyelids there, as I have done, retains the rather horrible and also comic aspect of scrutiny, whilst also conveying, through the image of the half closed female eyelid, the personal beauty aspect of the line, but in a way that is not a ready made phrase that would sit typically in the mouth of an English bore, but one that suits this rather dry character in *Creditors*. It is also the phrase Strindberg used, presumably for the same reason.

Also, Meyer inexplicably replaces Scandinavian cultural references with French ones. Karin Månesdotter becomes Joan of Arc, and 'it was shit as they say in Denmark' becomes: 'it was what the French call Merde' and so on. This happens often enough for one to get the impression that Strindberg was either French or English.

Meyer seems to believe that Strindberg would have liked to conform to the norms of British theatre and so he helps him by removing his idiosyncracies, and gives him a style more easily digestible to a British audience. But Strindberg has never been easily digestible, even to a Swedish audience, he has never been a decent chap, and had very little distance from his writing. For me, Meyer removes Strindberg's personality and in doing so makes it ultimately harder to understand some of the strange things contained in these plays.

It is fashionable to consider that Meyer's translations are dated, and any theatre that can afford it likes to commission a new one. This has spawned a frightening selection of frankly Philistine, substandard 'versions' or poor translations. It is worth noting that Meyer is only dated insofar as he tried to update or Anglicise Strindberg, and impose a generic 'good dialogue' style upon him. But in this Meyer is the least of all offenders.[1]

The late Kenneth MacCleish opts for a wild paraphrasing and completely alters Strindberg's style. His rule of thumb is to use as few words as possible and he sacrifices everything to brevity and briskness, which gives a peculiar sensation of inexplicable haste to each speech, as well as an admixture of crudeness, even clumsiness, altogether alien to Strindberg, and these translations clearly aim to satisfy the modern presumptions of what dialogue should be, rather than being any attempt to render Strindberg into English. Strindberg was generally direct, but he took his time to say what he wanted to say. He savoured his phrases and didn't have the lesser writer's fear of prolixity. Here he finds himself at odds with modern 'Translatorese', and the confusion of vulgarity or briskness with effectiveness.

Elizabeth Sprigge's translations into American are still available. These are broadly dependable but a bit discordant to English ears and would seem to us more Americanised than they would to Americans. Peter Watts translations from the 1930s are not at all bad but far less accurate than Michael Meyers which in general are a vast improvement in style also. Watts does have his moments however and makes a useful comparison but he sometimes makes obvious mistakes.

The Swede Eivor Martinus has strangely chosen to translate into a language not her own. It is difficult to see whether this is an absurd arrogance or misguidedness, but the result is an uncomfortable jumble of English idioms as if from a thesaurus, piled on top of one another, accompanied by some strange errors. The worst of it though is that she completely fails to capture Strindberg's style and manages somehow to make him sound like a middle-aged, middle-class, Swedish woman speaking English, a fate I am not sure he would relish.

These are the translators, the version writers are many: essentially they work from literal translations, or crib from Meyer perhaps, and then take their own particular shot in the dark, not caring about the target in any case, creating, as they do, something after their own mind. This is apparently acceptable these days. One notable failure was the National Theatre's invitation to John Osborne to 'do' *The Father*. The matching of reputations or personalities, being the master stroke, a literary managers daydream: the crude vulgar-tongued travesty of Strindberg's play, the result. It bore little resemblance to Strindberg's voice which was not audible. By this stage I doubt if anyone noticed or regretted his absence for the public is now used to a variety of inappropriate manifestations. There are even those to whom such an exercise is a triumph in which theatre folk demonstrate their right to liberate themselves from the tyranny of the playwright, or the play, and well, just do their own thing.

The British public's perception of Strindberg is based chiefly on *Miss Julie*, which is the most often performed of his plays. This is perhaps not surprising since it is the play where he exercises the naturalist principles outlined in his introduction (included here). These should be seen in their context, as a reaction to certain late nineteenth-century theatre practices in performance and writing. To us the points he mentions seem like common sense; an actor should employ real time in doing an action, should not mind turning his back to the audience, shouldn't proclaim and so on. It is surprising however how often one sees 'expressionist' productions ignoring the introduction Strindberg went to the trouble to attach to the play.

Most of Strindberg's plays are not written in anything that could be called a naturalistic style, although the dialogue is psychologically consistent with the characters which are usually convincingly drawn. Even in plays where he is most controlled by his misogynist demon, he manages surprisingly well to get inside the female characters even while he manipulates them wildly to confirm his thesis.

It is a shame that audiences are not very well acquainted with the strange atmosphere in much of Strindberg's writing as this is perhaps what is most attractive about it. Theatres tend to see him as a revolutionary hero, a role made problematic by his misogyny, and as a reformer of dramatic writing, although it is mostly his reform in the direction of naturalism which gets attention in this country. At any rate some translators try to give him the brisk style a revolutionary should have.

Strindberg's idiosyncrasies are of a far different nature. For a start he tended to write quickly and hated revising or even reading over what he had written. One can feel with him that indeed once he began to correct his excesses the whole thing would unravel. So he leaves it. Sometimes, as with *The Father*, he was surprised and horrified himself when he saw it on the stage. We might as well accept it warts and all. There are errors or repetitions and inconsistencies. Some translators have removed these (perhaps feeling they may get the blame). He writes confidently and fluently, inventing some words, taking liberties with grammar, using, in short the language as it suits him. He has a wide and sometimes quaint vocabulary which can be surprising and funny. He doesn't write the kind of dialogue we have learnt from the television and we shouldn't try to make it fit our expectations.

It may be worth noting that his style is very different from Ibsen's whose actual speeches tend to be plainer and simpler, and to have a more everyday feel. Ibsen is essentially poetical in his technique, and the beauty of his plays is how the splitting of doom reverberates through his characters words and actions, a lyrical *deus ex machina*. In Strindberg the characters themselves take a very active role in presenting the concerns of the play, they argue, accuse and describe their experience and interpretations of life. This gives the dialogue an almost constant dialectical, rather anguished tone. The language itself has a consequent hard formality. The anger is of the kind that needs to prove its point and that aggravates itself whilst doing so, bewildered by the success of its self-justification. At its most vigourous it verges on pomposity which sometimes manifests itself in rather stiff formulations. Translators shy away from this – it seems ungraceful and doesn't resemble the smooth-flowing modern dialogue we haver learned to expect. But it is nevertheless part of the way Strindberg writes.

The Father

The Father was written just before *Miss Julie*. It concerns a father's struggle with his wife over the upbringing of their daughter. The father perceives that there is a conspiracy in the household against him, including his wife's mother. This seems to be a fixed idea which drives him mad. His wife, believing her own lies, manipulates events to enable her to win the battle and get her own way, finally arranging for her husband to be put in a straight jacket.

In one sense the play is about what it is to be a man, more especially a father, naturally a problematic role for he is in a sense the least important of the parental pair. Here the central character is, like other of Strindberg's males, torn between the masculine and feminine side of his own nature. Strindberg wrote it whilst living in Germany and apparently became fascinated with the militarism there. So the hero in this play is a cavalry officer. In one speech he complains of the constraints which expectations of masculinity put upon a man's nature and his need to express his feelings.

The complete collapse of this character – he ends up in the arms of his old wet-nurse – seems to be caused by his strong paternal instinct to protect his child and his inability to come to terms with her mother, so that he finally doubts that he is the child's father, something he claims a man can never be sure of. He is driven from his reason by the apparent gulf between a woman's way of thinking and his own – whilst at the same time yearning partly to be freed from his manhood. It is perhaps appropriate that the part of his wife is drawn somewhat sketchily since she is incidental to the man's internal struggle, and really only a projection of his own femininity. What is noticable is that the writer has no greater objectivity regarding the character of the woman than does the man himself, so that when she is shown on her own, or talking to another character, she still has the same shallow, scheming nature. In fact she is more rounded when she is in scenes with the man. This identification with the central male character at the expense of the others is a distinctive feature of Strindberg's writing. Obviously it undermines its scope, whilst in some way increasing its intensity, that is he is not writing about paranoid feelings, but being paranoid. Any chink in the curtain of self-absorbtion always comes as a surprise, and an encouragement, just at the point perhaps when one may be asking oneself if there is any point in reading it. We are used to writers having a quite particular view of the world, and we like it, or at least suspend our disbelief temporarily, before we forget it all and go back to our lives, in the hope or suspicion that the view they have may be a clearer or even a better one than our own, and may throw some light onto hitherto obscure areas, or merely confirm half-thought thoughts of our own, bringing us relief and comfort and encouragement. None of this is quite the case with Strindberg, at least not directly. Much of the time we feel that his view is inferior to our own, more narrow and blind than is even normal. Largely this is because of his attitude to women. Perhaps he would have been a far better writer if he was not consumed with suspicion and fear, if his brain wasn't made feverish with irascibility. The force with which he describes his vision is in a sense the main feature of his writing rather than the vision itself. The very fact that a man has such a distinct vision of the world, where each detail conspires to reinforce the unhappy circumstances of a sometimes hateful present, reverberates strongly with us, largely because it is hard to ignore someone who is so intensely alive. They remind us what life is. Strindberg's response to being so hard done by at the hands of the women is not cold dissociation, itself a very common human response, but a passionate or rather desperate panic, which motivates him to seek ever further proofs and justifications to the point where we eventually laugh or throw the book away in disgust. What is interesting about him though is not the bit we call mad (for madness itself is pretty dull, as is his), but rather the great effort he makes to retain his sanity. He clings on desperately to the world we all inhabit, tries to make himself master of it sometimes, like any great poet, or like anyone who makes himself an inhabitant of the world as a whole. He suceeds when he is aware of the scale of Truth, of the spirits good and bad which follow us through our lives. In this way his scope is broad, and I think there is a particular effect created by achieving such a scope whilst battling against a heart seized in a constricting grip. Perhaps it is this which makes Strindberg so familiar and appealing to the reader.

Miss Julie

Miss Julie is a tense drama more or less observing the unities, concerning the mutual seduction of a servant and his master's daughter, one midsummer's eve. The battle, for so it is, between the protagonists, is fought over two terrains – gender and class difference – and rarely if ever do either of the characters say or do anything which is not attributable to these causes, or at least interpreted by the other as being so. This adds to the overheated claustrophobic sensation one gets from the play, and is part of its rigourous power, although it doesn't make it one of Strindberg's most inspiring works, rather one which suits contemporary theatre's enthusiasm for polemic. Where Strindberg succeeds so well is that notwithstanding the above, the drama seems to be driven by a desperate humanity that is subsumed by the gender and class. If this is a tragedy, and Strindberg said it was, it is perhaps because it shows how difficult it can be for human beings to free themselves from the social forces which form them, or even to have the will to do so. Whenever these two try they fail; either because it is simply impossible; or because the other won't let them, but would rather blame and chastise, as if the desire for satisfaction were too strong; or lastly, because Strindberg can't let them, for his own anger and frustration prevents him. The spectacle of these two potential lovers having their noses rubbed in their own blood and sweat respectively is the opposite of edifying.

The Comrades[2]

The Comrades concerns a modern marriage where the participants are not so much man and wife as friends, partners in an enterprise. Strindberg takes a very modern notion and reveals the bad side of it. People like to think of Strindberg as a radical – well here he shoves himself so much ahead of his time as to be able to have a reactionary response to things that hadn't really happened yet. Is Strindberg annoyed by the clumsy attempts at equality of his female contemporaries, including his wife, or is it the shallowness of some of the manifestations of moderness which he abhors?

On one level it is easy to see that Strindberg has clearly an intolerant nature. The same intolerance serves to make him impatient with the inequities of his day, and makes him furious at the sight of the forcibly weaker half of society flexing inexpertly its underdeveloped muscles. It strikes him as incongruous. He prefers the underdog to be a strong one. Or perhaps he fears women precisely for their strengths. He certainly fears them, 'those chronic anaemics haemorrhaging thirteen times a year'.

These plays, as well as later ones, are full of fantasised descriptions of scheming women who resort to underhand tactics because of their inherent inferiority – to destroy the man. It's not hard to despise Strindberg's position. He protests too much, and shows terrible personal weakness.

In a sense what redeems the plays is when the weakness is central. In *The Father* and in *Creditors* the weak hysterical man is driven to despair by his inability to cope with women, who generally exhibit little more in the way of faults than a little stubbornness or selfishness, a quaint tendency to twist the truth on trivial matters, and nothing to rival the man in this area, who twists the facts into a kind of perverted religion of disappointed manhood. He is like a man who loses every argument because he doesn't know when to stop, taking everything too far and thereby losing every reasonable point he may have made along the way. We have the spectacle of him getting carried away, drowning finally in his own hypocrisy and pomposity. He makes the mistake of thinking that just because his brain supplies him with a mesh of connecting points to support his thesis, a mesh which grows about him, that these points must necessarily be true and that this is proved by the way they all connect up. He ends enmeshed in spuriousness.

It is this quality of Strindberg's mind, the ability to make connections, that makes him a good playwright – when it is working expansively rather than reductively. It is an ability by the way, Ibsen also has. With Ibsen, when it works in the realm of intellectual ideas, it is less exciting than when it works in his unconscious and gives the plays that terrible sense of the dead hand of destiny that makes his later, less polemical plays so remarkable (and so frightening to British directors who are embarrassed by them).

Joyce admired this quality in Ibsen, and of course he also had this propensity to multiply connections to a mind-shattering degree. It has to do with the aesthetic requirement, which he states in *Portrait of the Artist as a Young Man*, that each part of a piece of art should contribute to the whole and furthermore contain the pattern of the whole within it. One needn't agree with this to see that it is applicable to much of what is good art, though not all perhaps, and absent from most of what is poor.

Strindberg has this quality, so that even when his writing is below par it is still compelling. Even *The Pelican*, a pretty dreadful play in many respects, holds together quite hypnotically, while in *The Dream Play*, *Easter* or *Ghost Sonata* it allows Strindberg to draw sometimes disparate strands into a coherent and complete seeming world.

In *Miss Julie* it is the man who has strength through a shallowness usually found in the women characters. It is perhaps interesting that in this, his most performed play, the characters are on the whole for him atypical, as is the highly controlled tone of the writing. In comparison to the rest of his work, one cannot help feeling that it is the play's very conventionality in modern terms, which is its appeal to today's theatre-folk.

In *The Comrades* a man has found himself in a rather self-consciously 'modern' style relationship where there is much made of the way the finances are held, and the fact that both partners are painters and have equal rights to pursue their careers. The couple have fashionable friends, among them a feminist who doesn't like men at all it seems, and who is a bit of an influence on the wife. Eventually the man finds the whole thing intolerable, largely because his wife is a selfish and mean-spirited creature who manipulates things to her supposed advantage, is disloyal to old friends out of misplaced militancy, and a poor painter to boot who doesn't realise it. The denouement of the play, accompanied by a rough show of male physical strength over the woman, is that the husband sees the light and walks out on this marriage that is not a marriage. It is not a marriage because his wife is too busy trying to be a man, something she can never be, while needlessly rejecting her husband's attempts to fulfil his role which he does out of the purest motives. The general sense of the thing is that if the sexes would settle down to the roles given them, there would be more room, within that framework, random though it might or might not be, for a genuine loving relationship, based on mutual respect (the kind of relationship their friend Carl and his wife have). One might say that the argument is for simplicity and naturalness in relationships, and that the play is a satire upon the awkwardness of too deliberate arrangements providing formal equality between the sexes. But it is disingenuous to pretend that this equality needs to be the subject of incongruous arrangements. Strindberg seems to be starting from a premise that gender equality is unnatural in itself.

If there is a feminist looking for a play to beat Strindberg over the head with, she, or he, need look no further. It's all here, including a rather convincing, but incomplete, argument as to why women should keep out of the arts.

This is a comedy which is undermined by the way the thesis grows larger and finally dominates; dogmatism is a joke spoiler as well as a passion killer, and perhaps Strindberg's work and life suffered from both effects respectively. The humour of seeing the woman taking up her 'distressed' posture on the sofa when she thinks no one can see her is ruined when we feel just how much Strindberg wants to prove his point. To be really funny there must be some ambiguity, or at least surprised expectations, and here there are none, except in the smaller details, such as the pretentious Misses Hall with their dirty past in Petersburg. The character of the feminist is really quite sympathetically drawn, or at least quite rounded, except when Strindberg makes her say that what she really would admire is a man who had the guts to put a woman in her place, that place being beneath him. What is, I think, genuinely enjoyable about this play is the rare chance to see the so-called avant-garde lifestyle described for a change by someone who is neither enthusiastic nor impressed, but who is instead plagued by it and horrified. A bit of rotten apple from the horse's mouth, the reluctant insider's view.

Creditors

This is perhaps the most balanced or ambiguous in this collection of plays concerning relations between the sexes. Gustav, Tekla's ex-husband turns up and, incognito, inveigles his way into the new husband Adolf's confidences as a way of shattering the new relationship. The play is neatly set in a spa hotel room and is a very effective comedy, wickedly funny in that there is a sadistic or maybe masochistic pleasure in seeing the victim so effectively worked upon. This is a very good play for actors, having three very good parts, and for audiences too who are made a party to what is going on throughout. It is surprising this doesn't turn up in commercial theatres more often than it does.

Unusually for Strindberg in these matters, one isn't quite sure who's side he's on. Even Tekla, the incorrigible flirt, has her justifications and is found to be essentially innocent and sincere. Adolf, the new husband, is the familiar man-on-the-rack, driven there by his capricious wife's hints at infidelity. He manifests the kind of weaknesses in his personality that destroy his namesake in *The Father*, allowing himself to be influenced in every particular by his new 'friend' Gustav, who even persuades him to give up painting for sculpture. At the same time Adolf has it pointed out to him that it is in a woman's nature to absorb the opinions of the man she loves – what does this make Adolf who is so easily reformed by his new friend? Another womanly man? Indeed this character is so soft-centred as to lack the kind of charm one might imagine necessary to conquer a woman like Tekla, and we tend to believe Gutav's assertion that their relationship is built upon a kind of infantilism. To the extent that Strindberg is depicting himself in Adolf, this is self-laceration. (But we need not go too far in presuming this: writers generally use themselves to write the play rather than using the play to write themselves – the play is the thing, contrary to common deconstruction credo.) Strindberg could find both characters in himself so we can find him in both of them if we want to. Like Adolf, Strindberg took another man's wife away from him and probably had some trouble ridding his conscience of the ghost. Here Gustav comes back for revenge after being publicly dubbed an 'idiot' and as avenging victims sometimes do, he seems to know, like Banquo, what is spoiling his target's enjoyment of the fruits of their usurpation. A projection, we might say, where Gustav is an aspect of Adolf. Certainly Strindberg commutes easily between his sympathies for the two, but gives the upper hand always to Gustav, the strong type of man he might like to be, while at the same time allowing Tekla to point out what an essentially shallow nature such a man must have. She rejects him, after of course allowing him to seduce her. The initial success of the seduction is significant and is probably what most makes the play appeal to the 'realistic' preferences of the modern audiences, over the 'romantic'. It's still quite a tough pill to swallow when it comes. I imagine both female and male readers, except those hardy souls who identify with Gustav, are hoping that Tekla won't fall for it – although for different reasons. The men because they hope women aren't like that, the women if they resent the suggestion that they are. Gustav is only made powerful by the moral weaknesses of his victims. Although he is a bit of a villain, he carries some useful warnings to hypocrites.

One of the chief pleasures is just how thoroughly Strindberg does the job. Adolf is destroyed in his heart and his soul, in his intellect and in his body, he is reduced literally to epilepsy and celibacy, infancy and jealousy, and along the way he is mocked for his weak-minded atheism which sets up his wife to be worshipped because he 'must worship something'.

Strindberg has dipped his hand into his troubled heart and produced a pretty sharp comedy. He is often at his best in a satirical mood since this ensures that the plague falls on both houses.

Gregory Motton
London, 2000

---

[1] For Meyer on top form try to get a copy of his excellent translation of *No*, a comedy by the Danish nineteenth century playwright Hedberg.

[2] This title *Kamraterna* is difficult to translate and frankly I am not pleased with *The Comrades*, or the other alternative, *The Friends*. *Kamraterna* actually means rather the friends; comrades has a rather Soviet feel to it which is not at all present. A child has 'kamrater' in Sweden, playmates. However I felt both friends and any other variation of it, (pals, playmates etc.) to sound rather silly as a title, like either a sitcom or an American musical, so I stuck to *The Comrades*, by which it is generally known in English.

THE FATHER

Fadren

a tragedy in three acts

(1887)

Characters

CAPTAIN

LAURA

BERTHA

DOCTOR ÖSTERMARK

PASTOR

NÖJD

BATMAN

NURSE

Note on pronunciation of character's names:
BERTHA: 'batt-a'
ÖSTERMARK: 'ö' as in french 'oeuf'
NÖJD: 'öj' as in french 'oeuil'

ACT ONE

A living room in the CAPTAIN's house. A door upstage right. In the centre of the room, a large round table with newspapers and journals. To the right a leather sofa and a table. In the right hand corner a jib-door. On the left a bureau with an ornamental clock upon it; a door to the rest of the apartment. Weapons are upon the walls; rifles and game bags. Coat-hangers by the door with military coats upon them. On the large table a lamp burning.

Scene 1

The CAPTAIN and the PASTOR sit on the leather sofa. The CAPTAIN wears fatigues and riding boots with spurs. The PASTOR is dressed in black, with a white cravat, but no priest's collar; he smokes a pipe.

The CAPTAIN rings.

BATMAN: Yes sir?

CAPTAIN: Is Nöjd out there?

BATMAN: Nöjd is awaiting your orders in the kitchen.

CAPTAIN: Is he in the kitchen again! Send him in immediately!

BATMAN: At once, Captain. (*Goes.*)

PASTOR: What's the row this time?

CAPTAIN: That rascal's been interfering with the maid again. The boy's a damn nuisance!

PASTOR: Nöjd? He was in trouble last year too!

CAPTAIN: Yes, you remember that! But wouldn't you do me a favour and say a few friendly words to him, it may sink in better. I've sworn at him, and I've thrashed him, but it doesn't work.

PASTOR: So, you want me to preach to him. What effect do you think the word of God has on a cavalryman.

CAPTAIN: Well, brother-in-law, it doesn't have much effect on me, you know that...

PASTOR: I certainly do!

CAPTAIN: But with him! Try in any case.

Scene 2

As before. NÖJD.

CAPTAIN: What have been up to now, Nöjd?

NÖJD: God bless you Captain sir, I can't say, not with the Pastor present.

PASTOR: Don't be embarrassed now, my boy!

CAPTAIN: Own up now, otherwise you know what will happen.

NÖJD: Yeah, well, you see, we were at a dance at Gabriel's, and then, well like, Ludvig said...

CAPTAIN: What has Ludvig got to do with it? Stick to the truth.

NÖJD: Yeah, and then Emma said we should go out to the barn.

CAPTAIN: I see, so it was Emma who seduced you?

NÖJD: Yes, not far off. And I will say this, if the girl doesn't want it, there won't be any.

CAPTAIN: Get to the point: are you the father of the child or not?

NÖJD: How can a fellow know that?

CAPTAIN: What? Don't you know?

NÖJD: No, because you can't ever know that, see.

CAPTAIN: Weren't you alone then?

NÖJD: Yeah that time I was, but you still can't know if you're the only one?

CAPTAIN: Are you trying to blame Ludvig? Is that what you mean?

NÖJD: It's not easy to say who's to blame.

CAPTAIN: Yes, but you have said to Emma that you want to marry her.

NÖJD: Yeah, well you always have to say that...

CAPTAIN: (*To the PASTOR.*) It's dreadful isn't it!

PASTOR: Familiar stuff all this! But listen, Nöjd, you must be man enough anyway to know if you're the father or not?

NÖJD: Yes, I was in there right enough, but as you know yourself Pastor, there needn't be anything come of it!

PASTOR: Listen my boy, it's you we're talking about now! And you don't want to leave the girl on her own with the child! No one can force you to marry, but you've got to take care of that child! You must!

NÖJD: Yes, but Ludvig has to help in that case.

CAPTAIN: Then it'll have to go to the courts. I can't sort all this out, and I really can't be bothered either. Quick, march!

PASTOR: Nöjd! A word. Mm. Don't you think it dishonourable to leave a girl high and dry like that with a child? Don't you think so? Eh! Don't you consider such a way of going about things to be...em, em...

NÖJD: Yeah, well if I knew I was the father of the child, but you see you can never know that, Pastor. And slaving all your life to support someone else's child is no joke! I'm sure you Pastor and the Captain can appreciate that yourselves!

CAPTAIN: Quick march!

NÖJD: God bless you, Captain. (*Goes.*)

CAPTAIN: But don't go into the kitchen you scoundrel!

Scene 3

The CAPTAIN and the PASTOR.

CAPTAIN: Well, why didn't you pitch into him!

PASTOR: What? Didn't I tell him?

CAPTAIN: Ah, you just sat there mumbling to yourself!

PASTOR: Quite honestly, I don't know what to say. It's hard on the girl, yes; it's hard on the boy, yes. Suppose he's not the father! The girl can breastfeed the baby for four months in the orphanage and then the child is taken care of, but the boy can't breastfeed. The girl gets a good position in a decent house, but the boy's future could be ruined, if he's discharged from the regiment.

CAPTAIN: Yes upon my soul I wouldn't like to be in the magistrate's shoes and have to judge in this case. The boy isn't completely innocent, we can't be sure, but one thing you can be sure of: and that is the girl is guilty, if we are to say anyone is guilty.

PASTOR: Yes, yes! I judge no one! But what were we talking about, before this blessed episode came and interrupted us. It was about Bertha's confirmation, wasn't it?

CAPTAIN: Yes but it wasn't really about her confirmation, but rather her whole upbringing. This house is full of women, all of whom want to bring up my child. My mother-in-law wants to turn her into a spiritualist; Laura would have her be an artist; the governess wants to turn her into a Methodist; old Margret would have her a Baptist; and the maids want her in the Salvation Army. And of course you can't patch together a person's soul in that way, meanwhile I, who have the right to guide her nature, am endlessly opposed in my endeavours. I must get her away from this house.

PASTOR: You've too many women, in charge here.

CAPTAIN: Yes, haven't I just! It's like being in a cage full of tigers, and if I don't keep my red-hot iron right under their noses, they'd tear me to pieces in a second! Yes you laugh, you rogue. It wasn't enough that I took your sister to wife, you had to trick me into taking your old step-mother off your hands as well.

PASTOR: Well good God, a man really doesn't want a stepmother in his home.

CAPTAIN: No, but you think mothers-in-law are better kept in someone else's house, of course.

PASTOR: Yes yes, well and each has his burden to carry.

CAPTAIN: Yes, but I've got decidedly too much. I've got my old nanny as well, who treats me as if I'm still wearing a bib. She's very kind, God knows, but she doesn't belong here!

PASTOR: My dear brother-in-law, you've got to keep control of the womenfolk; you let them rule you all too much.

CAPTAIN: Listen, can you inform me just how one is meant to keep control of these women.

PASTOR: Strictly speaking, Laura, my own sister I know, was always somewhat difficult.

CAPTAIN: Laura does have a difficult side to her, but with her it's not so bad.

PASTOR: Oh, come on, be honest, I know her.

CAPTAIN: She's had a romantic upbringing and she has a little difficulty finding herself, but after all she is my wife...

PASTOR: And just because she is your wife, you think she's the best. No, it's her, putting the squeeze on you most.

CAPTAIN: Well, in any case, the whole house is in uproar. Laura won't let Bertha out of her sight, and I can't let her stay in this madhouse!

PASTOR: So, Laura says no; then, I fear great difficulties. When she was a child, she used to play dead, until she got her own way, and then when she got what she wanted, if it was an object, she'd give it back with the explanation that it wasn't the thing she wanted, but only to get her own way.

CAPTAIN: I see, so she was like that already. Mm! She certainly gets into such passions sometimes, that she worries me and I think she's ill.

PASTOR: But what is it now that you want for Bertha that is so unreasonable? Can't there be a compromise?

CAPTAIN: You mustn't think that I want to make her into a prodigy or into an image of myself. I don't want to be a matchmaker to my own daughter and bring her up solely for marriage, because if she were then to remain unmarried, she would suffer a bitter life. But I don't on the other hand want to guide her toward a masculine career, which requires a long training and the long preparation, which would be thrown away and wasted if she should marry.

PASTOR: What do you want then?

CAPTAIN: I want her to become a teacher. If she remains unmarried, then she can earn her living and be no worse off than these poor teachers, who have to use their salary to support a family. If she marries, she can use her knowledge bringing up her own children. That makes sense doesn't it?

PASTOR: That's right! But has she on the other hand shown such an ability for painting that it would be a crime against nature to suppress it?

CAPTAIN: No! I have shown her efforts to an eminent painter, and he says that it's just the kind of stuff you get in any art school. But then this young whippersnapper arrives this summer, who knows better, and says she has a great talent, and that decides everything in Laura's favour.

PASTOR: Was he in love with the girl?

CAPTAIN: I take that completely for granted!

PASTOR: God be with you then my boy, because I can see nothing that can be done. But it is bad, and of course Laura has support...in there.

CAPTAIN: Yeah, you can depend on it! The house is all ablaze with it, and between you and me it's not exactly a noble struggle being fought from their side.

PASTOR: (*Gets up.*) Don't you think I'm familiar with it?

CAPTAIN: You too?

PASTOR: Me too?

CAPTAIN: But the worst is, that it seems to me, Bertha's career is being determined, in there, by hateful motives. They go about proclaiming that men will see, that women can do this and do that. It's men against women endlessly, all day. – Are you going? No, stay the evening. I've nothing to offer you of course in the way of hospitality, but nevertheless; you know I'm expecting the new doctor to arrive. Have you seen him?

PASTOR: I caught a glimpse of him, as I drove past. He seemed a decent and steady sort.

CAPTAIN: Well, that's good. Do you think he could be an ally for me?

PASTOR: Who knows? It depends how much time he's spent with women.

CAPTAIN: No, but won't you stay?

PASTOR: No thanks, dear boy, I promised to come home this evening and my wife gets so worried, if I'm late.

CAPTAIN: Worried? Angry, you mean! Well, as you will. Let me help you on with your fur.

PASTOR: It's certainly a very cold evening. Thank you. Mind your health, Adolf, you seem so nervous!

CAPTAIN: Do I seem nervous?

PASTOR: Yes, aren't you very well?

CAPTAIN: Is it Laura has given you that idea? For twenty years she has treated me as a potential corpse.

PASTOR: Laura? No, but, but you worry me. Look after yourself! That's my advice! Goodbye, old fellow; but didn't you want to talk about that confirmation?

CAPTAIN: Not at all! I assure you that business can progress its own merry way on the official bill of conscience. I'm no martyr to the truth. That's all behind us. *Adieu.* Send my regards!

PASTOR: *Adieu,* my brother. Say hello to Laura!

Scene 4

The CAPTAIN. LAURA enters.

CAPTAIN: (*Opens the desk of his bureau and sits down, adding up.*) Thirty-four – nine, forty-three – seven, eight, fifty-six.

LAURA: (*Comes in from apartment.*) Would you mind...

CAPTAIN: One minute! – Sixty-six, seventy-one, eighty-four, eighty-nine, ninety-two, one hundred. What is it?

LAURA: Maybe I'm disturbing you.

CAPTAIN: Not at all! Housekeeping money am I right?

LAURA: Yes, the housekeeping money.

CAPTAIN: Put the bills there, and I'll go through them.

LAURA: Bills?

CAPTAIN: Yes!

LAURA: Bills now is it?

CAPTAIN: Naturally, bills. The household affairs are on an unsteady footing, and in the event of a dispute, there must be bills otherwise one could be punished for negligence.

LAURA: If the household's affairs are in a bad state, then it's not my fault.

CAPTAIN: That's just what could be ascertained from the bills.

LAURA: If the tenant doesn't pay it's not my fault.

CAPTAIN: Who recommended the tenant so warmly? You! Why did you recommend that – what shall we call him – idler?

LAURA: Why did you accept that idler then?

CAPTAIN: Because I was not allowed to eat in peace, sleep in peace, or work in peace before you got him in here. You wanted him, because your brother wanted to get rid of him, your mother wanted him, because I didn't want him, the governess wanted him, because he was a preacher, and old Margret because she'd known his grandmother from childhood. That's why he was accepted; and if I hadn't taken him on then I would be in either the madhouse or the family grave. Meanwhile, here is the housekeeping and your pin money. You can give me the bills later.

LAURA: (*Curtseys.*) Thank you very much! – Do you keep accounts for what you spend other than on the household?

CAPTAIN: That doesn't concern you.

LAURA: No that's true, just as my child's upbringing isn't supposed to concern me. Have the gentlemen come to their decision after this evening's plenary?

CAPTAIN: I had already made my decision, and it remained only for me to communicate it to the only friend the family and I have in common. Bertha will take rooms in town, she'll leave in two weeks' time.

LAURA: And in whose house will she be taking rooms, might I ask?

CAPTAIN: The lawyer, Sävberg[1].

LAURA: That freethinker.

CAPTAIN: Children must be brought up in keeping with the father's beliefs, according to correct law.

LAURA: And the mother has no say in the matter.

CAPTAIN: None at all! She has sold her birthright whole-sale, and traded them in for the man's duty to keep her and her children.

LAURA: So she has no rights over her children?

[1] Pronounced: 'sairv-barrie' ('g' is soft in Swedish)

CAPTAIN: No, none at all! Once you sell something, it's not customary to get it back again and still keep the money.

LAURA: But if the mother and father should decide together...

CAPTAIN: How would that be. I want her to live in town, you want her to live at home. Mathematically speaking she would end up at the railway station between town and here. It's an unsolvable problem! You see!

LAURA: Then it must be resolved by force! – What did Nöjd want here?

CAPTAIN: That's a military secret!

LAURA: That the whole kitchen knows about.

CAPTAIN: Then you ought to know it too!

LAURA: I do know it.

CAPTAIN: And have you reached a verdict?

LAURA: It's written in the law!

CAPTAIN: The law doesn't state who is the child's father.

LAURA: No, but one usually knows.

CAPTAIN: Wise men say you can never know.

LAURA: That's peculiar! Can't one know who is the child's father?

CAPTAIN: No, so it is claimed!

LAURA: That's peculiar! How then can the father have such rights over the child?

CAPTAIN: He has them only in the event that he takes upon himself the responsibility, or it is imposed upon him. And in a marriage there is of course no doubt of the parenthood.

LAURA: Is there no doubt?

CAPTAIN: No, I should hope not!

LAURA: Well, what if the wife has been unfaithful?

CAPTAIN: That is not the case here! Have you any further questions?

LAURA: None at all!

CAPTAIN: Then I am going up to my room, and if you would be so good as to inform me when the doctor arrives. (*He closes the desk of his bureau and gets up.*)

LAURA: Yes, sir!

CAPTAIN: (*Goes to the door right.*) As soon as he arrives, for I don't wish to be impolite. Do you understand me! (*Goes.*)

LAURA: I understand!

Scene 5

LAURA alone; looks at the banknotes in her hands.

MOTHER-IN-LAW: (*Voice from inside.*) Laura!

LAURA: Yes!

MOTHER-IN-LAW: Is my tea ready?

LAURA: (*By the door.*) Coming in a minute! (*Goes to outer door.*)

BATMAN: (*Comes in and announces.*) Dr Östermark.

DOCTOR: My good lady!

LAURA: (*Goes towards him offering her hand.*) Welcome Doctor! You are most welcome to our home. The Captain is out, but he'll be back soon.

DOCTOR: Please forgive me for coming so late, but I've already been out seeing patients.

LAURA: Do sit down, please!

DOCTOR: Thank you very much.

LAURA: Yes, we're all very poorly around here at the moment, but I hope you'll get along well anyway, and for us all alone out here in the country, it is so important to find a doctor who takes an interest in his patients; and of you, Doctor, I have heard so much good, that I am sure there will be the most cordial of relations between us.

DOCTOR: You're too kind, but I hope on the other hand that my visits won't too often be required of necessity. I trust your family is generally healthy and...

LAURA: Yes, we have fortunately had no acute illnesses, but nevertheless all is not as it should be.

DOCTOR: Is it not?

LAURA: Things are not, alas, as we should really want them.

DOCTOR: Oh! You alarm me!

LAURA: There are circumstances in a family, that one is constrained by honour and conscience to conceal from the world...

DOCTOR: Apart from one's doctor.

LAURA: That's why it's my painful duty to tell the whole truth right from the start.

DOCTOR: Can we not delay this conversation until I've had the honour of being introduced to the Captain?

LAURA: No! You must hear me first, before you meet him.

DOCTOR: This is about him then?

LAURA: It's about him, my poor beloved husband.

DOCTOR: You worry me, madam, and I do sympathise with your distress, believe me!

LAURA: (*Takes out handkerchief.*) My husband is mentally ill. Now you know all and can judge for yourself later.

DOCTOR: What did you say! I have read with admiration the Captain's remarkable dissertations on mineralogy, and I've always found in them a clear and strong intelligence.

LAURA: Really? It would gratify me if all his family here have been mistaken.

DOCTOR: But it could be that his psyche is disturbed in other areas. Please tell me about it!

LAURA: That is what we are afraid of too! You see, at times he has the most bizarre ideas, as any very learned man might have, if only they weren't so disturbing to the well-being of his whole family. For example he has this mania for buying all kinds of things.

DOCTOR: How disturbing; but what does he buy?

LAURA: Cartloads of books, he never reads.

DOCTOR: Well, that a learned man buys books isn't so very worrying.

LAURA: You don't believe what I'm telling you?

DOCTOR: Yes, my dear lady, I am convinced that you believe what you're saying is true.

LAURA: But is it reasonable that a person can see through a microscope what is happening on another planet?

DOCTOR: Does he say that he can?

LAURA: Yes, he does.

DOCTOR: Through a microscope?

LAURA: Through a microscope! Yes!

DOCTOR: That is disturbing, if that is the case!

LAURA: If that is the case! I see you have no confidence in me, Doctor, and I am sitting here initiating you into all the family secrets...

DOCTOR: My dear lady, I am honoured by the confidence you have in me, but as a doctor, I must investigate and examine, before I judge. Has the Captain shown any symptoms such as unpredictable mood swings or an erratic will?

LAURA: Has he? We've been married for twenty years and he hasn't once made up his mind without then changing it.

DOCTOR: Is he obstinate?

LAURA: He always wants his own way, but once he gets his way, he gives up and begs me to decide.

DOCTOR: That is disturbing and requires close observation. The will, you see, is the backbone of the mind; if it becomes injured then the mind falls apart.

LAURA: And God knows I have learned to satisfy his demands all these long, testing years. Oh, if you only knew what kind of a life I've struggled through at his side, if you only knew!

DOCTOR: My dear lady, your distress touches me deeply, and I promise to look into what can be done. I feel sorry for you with all my heart and I beg you to depend on me entirely. But after what I've heard, I must ask you one thing. Avoid stirring up thoughts that may upset the patient, because in a weak mind, they can quickly develop into monomania or fixed ideas. Do you understand?

LAURA: You mean to avoid awakening his suspicions!

DOCTOR: Precisely! Because a sick man can imagine all kinds of things, just because he is so susceptible.

LAURA: Yes! Then I do understand. Yes! – Yes!

(*A bell rings from the flat.*)

Excuse me, my mother wants to tell me something. One moment... Look, here's Adolf... (*Goes.*)

Scene 6

The DOCTOR. The CAPTAIN comes in through the jib-door.

CAPTAIN: Oh, you're here already, Doctor! Welcome. Welcome to our home!

DOCTOR: Captain! It's such a delight to make the acquaintance of such a renowned scientist.

CAPTAIN: I beg you, please. My duties don't leave me the time for any serious research, but nevertheless I think I'm on to a new discovery.

DOCTOR: Indeed!

CAPTAIN: You see I've put a meteorite through spectral analysis and I have found carbon traces of organic life! What do you say to that?

DOCTOR: Can you see that in the microscope?

CAPTAIN: No, dammit, in the spectroscope!

DOCTOR: The spectroscope! Pardon me! Well then, you'll soon be able to tell us what's going on in Jupiter!

CAPTAIN: Not what's happening, but what has happened. If only the blessed bookseller in Paris would send me the books I've ordered, but I think all the booksellers in the world have taken oath against me. Can you imagine that for two months not a single one of them has responded to my orders, letters, or abusive telegrams! It's driving me insane and I just can't understand it!

DOCTOR: Ah, common negligence I expect; and you needn't take it so badly.

CAPTAIN: No, but dammit, I'm not able to finish my thesis in time and I know someone in Berlin is working on the same thing. But we shouldn't be talking about this! But rather about you. Would you like to stay here, we have a small apartment in the wing, or would you like to live in the old official lodgings?

DOCTOR: As you prefer.

CAPTAIN: No, as you prefer! Do say which!

DOCTOR: Captain you must decide!

CAPTAIN: No, I can't decide. It's you who must say which you prefer. I have no preference. None at all!

DOCTOR: No, but I can't decide...

CAPTAIN: In the name of Jesus, say what it is you want. I have nothing to say in the matter, no preference, no wishes! Are you such a sop, that you don't know what you want! Speak up, or I'll get angry!

DOCTOR: If it's up to me, I'll stay here!

CAPTAIN: Good! – Thank you! – Oh! – Excuse me, Doctor, but there's nothing that torments me so much as to hear people utter their indifference.

(*Rings. The NURSE comes in.*)

So it's you, Margret. Now my friend, is the wing ready for the Doctor?

NURSE: Yes, Captain, it is!

CAPTAIN: All right! Then I won't keep you, Doctor, you must be tired. Farewell and again welcome; I'll see you tomorrow, I hope.

DOCTOR: Good evening, Captain!

CAPTAIN: And I presume my wife has let you know the state of things here so that you know more or less how the land lies.

DOCTOR: Your splendid wife has given me a few hints on things, that could be useful for the uninitiated to know. Good evening, Captain.

Scene 7

The CAPTAIN. The NURSE.

CAPTAIN: What is it, my old friend! Do you want something?

NURSE: Listen to me now, little Adolf.

CAPTAIN: Yes, speak out dear old Margret. You're the only one I can listen to, without going into spasms.

NURSE: Listen now Mister Adolf, couldn't you go halfway and make it up with your wife about the child. She is her mother after all...

CAPTAIN: And I'm her father, Margret!

NURSE: Well, well, well! A father has other things than his child, a mother has only her child.

CAPTAIN: Exactly, my dear. She has only one burden, but I have three, and I carry her burden. Don't you think that I would have had a different position in life than that of an old soldier if I hadn't had her and her children.

NURSE: Yes, that wasn't what I wanted to say.

CAPTAIN: No, I can believe it, because you want me to be in the wrong.

NURSE: Don't you think I want what's best for you?

CAPTAIN: Yes, my dear friend, I think you do, but you don't know what's best for me. You see, it's not enough to have given the child life, I also want to give it my soul.

NURSE: Yes, well, you see I don't understand all that. But I still think you ought to be able to come to an agreement.

CAPTAIN: You're not my friend, Margret!

NURSE: Me? Oh my lord, the things you say. Do you think I can forget that you were my child when you were little.

CAPTAIN: Well, my dear, have I forgotten it? You have been like a mother to me, you've given me your support so far, when everyone else has been against me, but now, when it really counts, you betray me and go over to the enemy.

NURSE: Enemy!

CAPTAIN: Yes, the enemy! You know very well how things are in this house, you've seen everything, from start to finish.

NURSE: I've seen all right! But my God, is it right two people should torture the life out of each other; two people who are otherwise so good and who mean each other well. Madam is never like that to me or to anyone else...

CAPTAIN: Just to me, I know. But I'm telling you now Margret, if you desert me, then it's a sin. Because now a web is being spun about me, and that doctor is not my friend!

NURSE: Oh, Mr Adolf you think the worst of everyone, but you see, that's because you don't have the true faith; yes, I can see that.

CAPTAIN: But you and the Baptists have found the only
true faith. So you're happy!

NURSE: Yes, well I'm not as unhappy as you, Mr Adolf!
If you would humble your heart you'd see that God
would bless you with love for your neighbour.

CAPTAIN: It's extraordinary, that as soon as you speak of
God and love, your voice grows so hard and your eyes
so hateful. No, Margret, you definitely don't have the
true faith.

NURSE: Yes, you can be proud and hard with your
learning, but it won't get you far when it really matters.

CAPTAIN: How arrogantly speaks the humble heart.
Certainly learning couldn't help animals like you!

NURSE: Shame on you! But old Margret still loves her big,
big boy the most, and he'll come running back like a
good boy, when there's stormy weather.

CAPTAIN: Margret! Forgive me, but please believe me,
there's no one here means me well, except you. Help me,
because I can feel something is going to happen. I don't
know what it is, but it's not right what's going on.
(*Screams from inside the flat.*)
What is it! Who is screaming!

Scene 8

As before. BERTHA comes in from the apartment.

BERTHA: Papa, Papa, help me! Save me!

CAPTAIN: What is it beloved child! Tell me!

BERTHA: Help me! I think she wants to hurt me!

CAPTAIN: Who wants to hurt you? Tell me! Tell me!

BERTHA: Grandma! But it was my fault, I played a trick
on her!

CAPTAIN: Tell me!

BERTHA: Yes but you mustn't say anything! Do you hear,
I beg you!

CAPTAIN: All right, just tell me what you did!
(*The NURSE goes.*)

BERTHA: Well! Each evening, she lights the lamp, and then she sits me at the table with a pen in my hand over a sheet of paper. And then she tells me the spirits are going to write.

CAPTAIN: What! And you didn't tell me about this!

BERTHA: I'm sorry, but I didn't dare, Grandma says that the spirits avenge themselves, if you tell. And then the pen writes, but I don't know if it's me. And sometimes it works, but sometimes it doesn't work at all. And when I get tired then it won't come, but then it has to come anyway. And this evening, I think I wrote well, but Grandma said it was from Stagnelius[1] and that I tricked her; and then she got really angry.

CAPTAIN: Do you believe spirits exist?

BERTHA: I don't know!

CAPTAIN: But I know they don't!

BERTHA: Grandma says Daddy doesn't understand and that you've got much worse things, that can see other planets.

CAPTAIN: She says that does she! She says that! What else does she say?

BERTHA: She says you can't do magic!

CAPTAIN: I never said I could either. You know what meteorites are! Yes, stones that have fallen from heavenly bodies. I examine them and see if they contain the same elements as the earth. That's all I can see.

BERTHA: But Grandma says there are things, that she can see, that you can't see.

CAPTAIN: Well she's lying!

BERTHA: But Grandma doesn't lie!

CAPTAIN: Why not?

BERTHA: Because then so does Mama!

CAPTAIN: Mm!

BERTHA: If you say that Mama lies, then I'll never believe you again!

CAPTAIN: I didn't say that, and so you had better believe me when I tell you, my beloved child, that your well-being and your future requires that you leave this house!

[1] Swedish romantic poet (1793–1820)

Would you like that? Would you like to go to town and learn something useful!

BERTHA: Oh yes, I'd love to go to town and get out of here! Go anywhere, as long as I can see you, sometimes, often. It's always so gloomy and horrible in there, like a winter night, but when you come, Papa, it's like throwing open the windows on a spring morning!

CAPTAIN: My beloved child! My darling!

BERTHA: But, Papa, you must be kind to Mama, do you hear; She cries so often!

CAPTAIN: Mm! – So you want to go to live in town?

BERTHA: Yes! Yes!

CAPTAIN: But if Mama doesn't want you to?

BERTHA: But she must!

CAPTAIN: But if she doesn't?

BERTHA: Yes, then I don't know what we shall do! But she must, she must!

CAPTAIN: Will you ask her?

BERTHA: You have to ask her ever so nicely, because she won't pay any attention to me!

CAPTAIN: Mm! – Well, if you want it and I want it, and she doesn't want it, what shall we do then?

BERTHA: Oh, then things would become difficult again! Why can't you both...

Scene 9

As before. LAURA.

LAURA: Aha, Bertha is here! So now we can perhaps hear her opinion, since her fate is to be decided.

CAPTAIN: The child can't very well have an informed opinion on how a girl's life is going to form itself, whereas we on the other hand, can more or less guess, since we have seen how a large number of girls' lives have turned out.

LAURA: But since we are of differing opinions, Bertha can decide.

CAPTAIN: No! I won't allow anyone to encroach on my rights, neither woman nor child. Bertha, leave us.
(*BERTHA goes out.*)

LAURA: You were afraid of her opinion, because you thought it would be to my advantage.

CAPTAIN: I know that she herself wants to leave home, but I also know, that you have the power to change her mind at will.

LAURA: Oh, am I so powerful!

CAPTAIN: Yes, you have a satanic power to get your will, but so does anyone who doesn't mind what means they use. How for example did you get rid of Doctor Nordling and bring in this new one?

LAURA: Yes, how did I do that?

CAPTAIN: You insulted the former, so that he went, and you got your brother to get this one appointed.

LAURA: Well, it was very simple and completely legal. Is Bertha going to go away now?

CAPTAIN: Yes, she'll leave within fourteen days.

LAURA: Is that your decision?

CAPTAIN: Yes!

LAURA: Have you spoken to Bertha about it?

CAPTAIN: Yes!

LAURA: Then I shall have to try to prevent it!

CAPTAIN: You can't!

LAURA: Can't I! Do you think a mother would let her child out amongst bad people, so she can learn that everything her mother taught her is nonsense, so she can be despised by her daughter for the rest of her life.

CAPTAIN: Do you think a father can allow ignorant and conceited women to teach his daughter that her father is a charlatan?

LAURA: That shouldn't matter so much to the father.

CAPTAIN: Why is that?

LAURA: Because the mother is closer to the child, since someone has discovered that no one can really know who is the child's father.

CAPTAIN: What relevance has that in this case?

LAURA: You don't know if Bertha is your child!

CAPTAIN: Don't I?

LAURA: No, you can't know what no one can know!

CAPTAIN: Are you joking?

LAURA: No, I'm only using your own teaching. Besides, how do you know I haven't been unfaithful?

CAPTAIN: I could believe many things about you, but not that, and neither do I believe you would tell me, if it were true.

LAURA: Imagine if I were prepared for anything, even to be cast out, despised, to keep control over my child, and that I am telling the truth, when I say: Bertha is my child, but not yours! Imagine...

CAPTAIN: Stop it!

LAURA: Imagine that: that would be an end to your authority!

CAPTAIN: After you had proved I'm not the father!

LAURA: That wouldn't be difficult! Would you like that?

CAPTAIN: Stop it!

LAURA: I would naturally only have to supply the name of the real father, give the place and the time for example –, When was Bertha born? – the third year after our marriage...

CAPTAIN: Stop it now! Or I'll...

LAURA: Or you'll what? We'll stop now! But think carefully about what you do and what you decide! And above all don't make a fool of yourself!

CAPTAIN: I think all this is extremely sad!

LAURA: Then the more of a fool you appear!

CAPTAIN: But not you!

LAURA: No, we've arranged things far better than that.

CAPTAIN: That's why it's impossible to fight you.

LAURA: Why allow yourself to fight with a superior opponent.

CAPTAIN: Superior?

LAURA: Yes! Strangely enough, but I can never look at a man, without feeling superior.

CAPTAIN: Well, this time you've met your match and you're never going to forget it.

LAURA: That will be interesting.

NURSE: (*Comes in.*) Dinner is served. Would you care to come and eat?

LAURA: With pleasure!

(*The CAPTAIN hangs back; sits in an armchair by the table next to the sofa.*)

Are you going to come and eat the evening meal?

CAPTAIN: No, thank you, I don't want anything!

LAURA: What! Are you upset?

CAPTAIN: No, but I'm not hungry.

LAURA: Come now, otherwise people will ask – awkward questions! – Please! – You won't, sit there then! (*Goes.*)

NURSE: Mr Adolf! What's all this now?

CAPTAIN: I don't know. Can you explain to me how you women can treat an old man as if he were a child!

NURSE: Well I don't know; but it's probably because all men great and small are born of women...

CAPTAIN: But no woman is born of a man. Yes, but I'm Bertha's father. Tell me, Margret, don't you think? Don't you?

NURSE: Oh God, how childish you are. Of course you are your own child's father. Come and eat now, and don't sit there and sulk! There! There, come on now!

CAPTAIN: (*Gets up.*) Get out woman! To hell with you all! Damned witches! (*Calls out the hall.*) Svärd! Svärd![1]

BATMAN: (*Comes in.*) Yes, Captain!

CAPTAIN: Harness the sleigh at once!

NURSE: Now Captain! Listen to me...

CAPTAIN: Get out woman! At once!

NURSE: God preserve us, what's going to happen now?

CAPTAIN: (*Takes up his hat and prepares to go out.*) Don't expect me home! before midnight! (*Goes.*)

NURSE: Jesus help us, what will come of all this?

End of Act One.

---

[1] Pronounced: 'ä' as in 'lad'

ACT TWO

Same set as before. Lamps burning on the table; it is night.

Scene 1

The DOCTOR. LAURA.

DOCTOR: From what I could find from our conversation, the matter is still not clearly proven. To start with you were mistaken, when you said that he came to his surprising conclusions about the heavenly bodies using a microscope. Now I hear from him that it was a spectroscope, so not only does he appear free from suspicion of mental disorder, but rather to be a great credit to science.

LAURA: Yes, but I never said that!

DOCTOR: Madam, I made a note of our conversation and I remember that I questioned you on that particular point, since I thought I had heard wrongly. One has to be scrupulous with such accusations, when it involves a man being certified.

LAURA: Certified.

DOCTOR: Yes, you must know that an insane person loses all their rights as a citizen and as a family man.

LAURA: No, I didn't know that.

DOCTOR: There is a further point, which seems suspicious to me. He spoke of his letters to booksellers being unanswered. Permit me to ask – have you, of misdirected goodwill, intercepted them?

LAURA: Yes I have. But it was my duty to protect the interests of the household, and I couldn't let him ruin us all unchecked.

DOCTOR: Forgive me, but I don't think you have considered the consequences of such an action. If he should discover your secret interference in his affairs, then his suspicions will be confirmed and they will grow like an avalanche. By doing that you have furthermore restricted his will and increased his impatience. Surely you know yourself how it crushes the spirit, to have your keenest wishes opposed, one's will thwarted.

LAURA: I do indeed.

DOCTOR: Well, you can judge how he must have felt.

LAURA: (*Gets up.*) It's midnight and he hasn't come home. I must begin to fear the worst.

DOCTOR: But tell me, what happened this evening after I left; I have to know everything.

LAURA: He was raving and had the most peculiar ideas. Can you imagine such a notion that he is not the father of his own child.

DOCTOR: That is peculiar. But how did he come upon that idea?

LAURA: I've no idea, unless it was when he was interrogating one of his men concerning a child's paternity, and I took the side of the girl involved, and he got carried away and said that no one could say who was the father of a child. God knows I did all I could to calm him, but now I think there's nothing to be done. (*Cries.*)

DOCTOR: This mustn't continue; something must be done, but without arousing his suspicion. Tell me, has the Captain had fancies like this before?

LAURA: Six years ago it was just the same situation, and he admitted himself, yes, in a letter he himself wrote to his doctor, that he feared for his reason.

DOCTOR: Well, well, well, this is a business with deep roots, of course, the sanctity of the family – and all that – I can't ask you about everything, I must keep myself to what is visible. What's done cannot be undone unfortunately, and the cure should have been applied earlier. – Where do you think he is now?

LAURA: I have no idea. But he has such wild notions these days.

DOCTOR: Would you like me to await his return? I could of course to avoid arousing his suspicions say that I was visiting your good mother who is unwell.

LAURA: Yes, that's a fine idea! But don't leave us, Doctor; if you knew how worried I am. But wouldn't it be better if you told him outright what you think of his condition.

DOCTOR: One never does that with the mentally ill, before they bring up the subject themselves, and only then in certain cases. It depends altogether on what turn the case takes. But we mustn't sit here; maybe I should withdraw to the adjacent room, so it seems less contrived.

LAURA: Yes, that's better, then Margret can sit here. She normally sits up, when he's out and she's the only one who has any power over him. (*Goes to door left.*) Margret, Margret!

NURSE: What is it, madam! Is the master home?

LAURA: No, but you must sit here and wait for him; and when he comes, you must tell him that my mother is ill and that the Doctor has come.

NURSE: Yes, don't worry; I'll see that everything will be all right.

LAURA: (*Opens the door to the flat.*) Would you step this way, Doctor.

DOCTOR: Madam!

Scene 2

NURSE: (*By the little table; picks up a book of psalms and glasses. Reads half aloud.*)
'A grievous and a wretched thing
is life, and soon is over.
Death's angel hovers all about us
and calls throughout the world:
Vanity, Vanity!'

'All souls on earth
fall to his wrath
and grief alone remains
to carve above the gaping tomb:
Vanity, Vanity.
All is Vanity.'

BERTHA: (*Comes in with coffee pot and embroidery; speaks quietly.*) Margret, can I sit with you? It's so horrid up there!

NURSE: Lord preserve us; is Miss Bertha up still?

BERTHA: I have to work on Papa's Christmas present. And I've brought something nice for you to eat!

NURSE: Yes, but my little angel, this won't do; Bertha you have to get up tomorrow; and it's past twelve o'clock.

BERTHA: Well, what does that matter. I don't dare sit alone upstairs, I think it's haunted.

NURSE: There you are; what did I say! Yes, mark my words, they aren't friendly spirits in this house. What did you hear?

BERTHA: You know what I heard? Someone singing in the attic.

NURSE: In the attic! At this time of night!

BERTHA: Yes, it was the saddest, saddest song I've ever heard. And it sounded as if it came from the little lumber room, where the cradle is, you know on the left...

NURSE: Oy, oy, oy! And such dreadful weather we're having tonight! I think the chimneys are about to be blown down.
 'What is life but grievous toil?
 Brief respite and great travail.
 What then at best is this our life.
 Nothing more at all than strife.'
 Yes, my dear child, God grant us a happy Christmas!

BERTHA: Margret, is it true Papa is sick?

NURSE: Yes, it seems he is!

BERTHA: Then we mustn't celebrate Christmas. But how can he be up when he's ill.

NURSE: Well my dear, he has the kind of illness where he can stay up. Shush, someone's walking about in the hall. Go to bed now and take out the coffee pot; otherwise the master will be angry.

BERTHA: (*Goes out with the tray.*) Good night, Margret!

NURSE: Good night, my child, God bless!

Scene 3

The NURSE. The CAPTAIN.

CAPTAIN: (*Removes his coat.*) Are you still up? Go to bed now!

NURSE: Oh, I just wanted to wait up...
(*The CAPTAIN lights a lamp; opens desk lid to bureau; sits at it and takes letters and newspaper from his pocket.*)
Mr Adolf?

CAPTAIN: What do you want?

NURSE: The old lady is ill. And the doctor is here.

CAPTAIN: Is it serious?

NURSE: No, I don't think so. It's just a cold.

CAPTAIN: (*Stands.*) Who was the father of your child, Margret?

NURSE: Oh, I've told you so many times, it was that good for nothing Johansson.

CAPTAIN: Are you sure it was him?

NURSE: No, but how childish; of course I'm sure, there was only him.

CAPTAIN: Yes, but was he sure he was the only one?
No, he couldn't be, but you could be sure. That's the difference.

NURSE: No, I don't see any difference.

CAPTAIN: No, you can't see it but the difference is there anyway! (*He turns the leaves of the photo album on the table.*) Do you think Bertha is like me? (*He looks at the portrait in the album.*)

NURSE: Yes, like two peas in a pod!

CAPTAIN: Did Johansson admit to being the father?

NURSE: Oh well, he was forced to, wasn't he.

CAPTAIN: It's terrible! – There's the Doctor!

Scene 4

The CAPTAIN and the NURSE. The DOCTOR comes in.

CAPTAIN: Good evening, Doctor. How is my mother-in-law?

DOCTOR: Oh, it's nothing serious; just a slight sprain in her left foot.

CAPTAIN: I thought Margret said it was a cold. There seems to be a difference of opinion over the matter. Go to bed, Margret!

(*She goes. Pause.*)

Do sit down, Doctor.

DOCTOR: (*Sits.*) Thank you!

CAPTAIN: Is it true that you get striped foals if you cross a zebra with a horse?

DOCTOR: (*Surprised.*) That's absolutely correct.

CAPTAIN: Is it true that the next lot of foals will also be striped even if you then cross the same mare with a stallion?

DOCTOR: That is also true.

CAPTAIN: Therefore under certain circumstances a stallion can be father to striped foals, and vice versa?

DOCTOR: Yes! Evidently.

CAPTAIN: Which is to say: the likeness between children and father prove nothing.

DOCTOR: Oh...

CAPTAIN: Which is to say: fatherhood cannot be proved.

DOCTOR: Er – Ahem...

CAPTAIN: You are a widower and have children?

DOCTOR: Ye-es...

CAPTAIN: Didn't you ever feel ridiculous as a father. I know nothing so comic as the sight of a father leading his child through the street, or to hear a father talk of his children. 'My wife's children,' he should say. Didn't you ever feel the falsehood of our position, didn't you ever have any twinges of doubt, I won't say suspicions because I presume as a gentleman that your wife was above suspicion?

DOCTOR: No, I certainly never had, but Captain, wasn't it Goethe said: 'One must accept one's children in good faith?'

CAPTAIN: Good faith, when a woman is concerned? That's risky.

DOCTOR: Ah, there are many types of women.

CAPTAIN: More recent research shows there to be only
one type! – When I was young, I was strong and – if I
may boast – handsome. I recall now only two
momentary impressions, which later gave me misgivings.
I was travelling once on a steamboat. I sat in the lounge
with some friends. The young waitress came and sat
opposite me, her face swollen with crying, and told us
her fiancé had been shipwrecked. We gave her our
condolences and I ordered champagne. After the second
glass, I touched her foot; after the fourth her knee, and
by morning, I had comforted her.

DOCTOR: Just a fly in winter!

CAPTAIN: Here's the second and its a fly in summer. I was
in Lysekil. There was a young woman, who had her
children with her, but her husband was in town. She was
religious, had extremely strong principles, lectured me
in morals, was completely honourable as I believe. I lent
her a book, two books; when she departed, she, unusually
enough, returned them. Three months later I found in
one of these books a visiting card with a fairly clear
declaration of love. It was fairly innocent, as innocent a
declaration of love as can come from a married woman
to a stranger who never made any advances. Here is the
moral. Don't trust too much!

DOCTOR: Nor too little either!

CAPTAIN: No, the right amount! But you see, Doctor, that
woman was so unconsciously villainous that she told her
husband of her passion for me. That's precisely the
danger, that they're unaware of their instinctive villainy.
That is a mitigating circumstance, but it cannot prevent
the judgement, only mitigate it!

DOCTOR: Captain, your thoughts are of a morbid nature
and you should beware of them.

CAPTAIN: You use the word 'morbid'. You see, all steam
boilers explode when the manometer reaches one
hundred, but one hundred isn't the same for all boilers;
you see? Meanwhile, you are here to keep an eye on me.
If I were not a man, I would have the right to accuse or

appeal, as it is cunningly called, then I could give you the whole diagnosis of my illness, and what's more its history, but unfortunately I am a man, and all that's left to me is like a Roman to lay my arms across my breast and hold my breath until I die. Good night!

DOCTOR: Captain! If you are ill, it is not dishonourable for you to tell me all about it. I must hear both sides!

CAPTAIN: It's quite enough to hear the one side, I should think.

DOCTOR: No, Captain. And you know, that when I heard Mrs Alving orating over her dead husband, I thought to myself: what a damned shame that the fellow is dead!

CAPTAIN: Do you think he would have spoken, had he been alive! And do you think that if any dead man rose up, he would be believed? Good night, Doctor! You can hear that I am calm, and you can go safely to bed!

DOCTOR: Good night then, Captain. I can no longer concern myself with this matter.

CAPTAIN: Are we enemies?

DOCTOR: Far from it. It's a pity though that we cannot be friends! Good night. (*Goes.*)

CAPTAIN: (*Follows the DOCTOR to the upstage door; goes to the drawer left, opens it slightly.*) Come in, and we can talk! I heard you standing there and listening.

Scene 5

LAURA comes in abashed. The CAPTAIN sits at the bureau desk.

CAPTAIN: It's late, but we must have this out. Sit down! (*Pause.*) I've been to the post office this evening and picked up some letters! From them I have learnt that you have withheld both ingoing and outgoing letters. The immediate consequence of which has been a waste of time that has destroyed the value of my work.

LAURA: It was good intentions on my part, because you were neglecting your job for this other work.

CAPTAIN: I'm sure it wasn't good intentions, because you were aware that one day, I would gain more honour from the other work than from my official duties, and you wanted most of all that I should not gain that credit, because it emphasised your insignificance. Therefore I have intercepted letters addressed to you.

LAURA: That was nobly done.

CAPTAIN: You see, you do think highly of me, as they call it. From these letters it appears you have for some time been turning all my former friends against me by encouraging a rumour concerning my mental health. And you have succeeded in your efforts, for now virtually no one thinks I'm sane, from the commanding officer down to the scullery maid. This is how it now stands regarding my illness: my reason is unaffected, as you know, so I am both able to carry out my professional duties and my obligations as a father. I still have power over my feelings, as long as my will remains undamaged; but you have gnawed at it and gnawed at it so that soon the cogs will fly loose and the whole mechanism will snap and start whizzing backwards. I don't want to appeal to your better feelings because these you lack, that is your strength, I appeal rather to your self-interest.

LAURA: Let's hear it?

CAPTAIN: Through your behaviour you have managed to provoke my distrustfulness, so that my judgement has become clouded, and my thoughts are wandering. This is the approach of madness you have been waiting for, and which can come at any moment. The question for you now is: is it more in your interest that I remain well rather than become unwell! Think about it! I collapse, I lose my job, and you are stuck. If I die, then my life insurance goes to you both. But, should I take my own life you get nothing. It is at least in your interests that I live out my life.

LAURA: Is this meant to be a trap?

CAPTAIN: Of course! It's up to you either to go round it or stick your head into it.

LAURA: You talk of killing yourself! You wouldn't do it!

CAPTAIN: Are you sure! Do you think a man can continue living, when he has nothing and no one to live for?

LAURA: You surrender then?

CAPTAIN: No, I'm proposing peace.

LAURA: The conditions?

CAPTAIN: That I am allowed to keep my sanity. Free me from my suspicions and I'll give up the fight.

LAURA: What suspicions?

CAPTAIN: Concerning Bertha's origins?

LAURA: Are there any suspicions about it?

CAPTAIN: Yes, for me there are; and you have aroused them.

LAURA: Me?

CAPTAIN: Yes, you have dropped them like henbane into my ear, and the circumstances have fostered their growth. Set me free from the uncertainty, tell me straight: this is how it is, and I forgive you in advance.

LAURA: I can't accept the guilt that isn't mine.

CAPTAIN: What does it matter to you, when you have the security that I won't divulge it. Do you think a man would go about and trumpet his own shame?

LAURA: If I say it is not as you say, then you gain no certainty, but if I say it is so, then you have certainty. Consequently you wish it were so.

CAPTAIN: Strangely enough yes, but it must be because the former cannot be proved, only the latter.

LAURA: Have you any grounds for your suspicions?

CAPTAIN: Yes and no!

LAURA: I think you wish to find me guilty, so that you can get rid of me and become sole master over our child. But you won't catch me in that snare.

CAPTAIN: Do you think I would want someone else's child if I had proof of your guilt.

LAURA: No, I'm sure you wouldn't, and that's why I realised you were lying just now, when you gave me your forgiveness in advance.

CAPTAIN: (*Stands.*) Laura, save me and my sanity. You don't understand what I'm saying. If the child isn't mine, then I have no rights over it and don't want any, and that

is all you want. Not so? Perhaps there is something else
you want, besides? You want power over the child, but
you want me to stay on and support you?

LAURA: Power, yes. What is all this life and death struggle
about other than power?

CAPTAIN: For me, one who has no belief in life after death,
my child was my life after death. It was my picture of
eternity, and perhaps the only one that corresponds at all
to reality. If you take it away from me, then you sever
my life.

LAURA: Why didn't we separate in time?

CAPTAIN: Because the child bound us together; but bonds
became chains. And how did that happen? How? I have
never thought about it properly, but now my memory
stirs accusations, judgements perhaps. We'd been married
two years and had no children, you know best why that
was. I fell sick and lay dying. In an unfeverish moment
I hear voices in the living room. It was you and the
lawyer, talking about my wealth, which I still had then.
He was explaining that you could inherit nothing since
we had no children, and he asks you if you are with
child, and what you answered I never heard. I recovered,
and we had a child. Who is the father?

LAURA: You!

CAPTAIN: No, I'm not! There's a crime buried here that's
beginning to reek. And what a damnable crime! You
released the black slaves out of the kindness of your
heart, but you've kept the white ones. I worked and
slaved for you, your child, your mother, your servants;
I've sacrificed my career and promotion, I've undergone
torture, whipping, sleeplessness, and worry for your
upkeep, until my hair has gone grey; all so that you can
have the pleasure of a life free from care and when you
get old enjoy new life through your child. All this I
endured without complaint, because I thought I was
father to this child. This is the basest kind of theft, the
most brutal enslavement. I have had seventeen years of
enforced labour and I was innocent. How can you pay
that back?

LAURA: Now you've gone completely mad!

CAPTAIN: (*Sits.*) That's what you hope for! And I've seen how you have strived to conceal your crime. I pitied you because I didn't understand your sorrow, I have often calmed your bad conscience with caresses, thinking I was chasing away morbid thoughts; I have heard you cry out in your sleep and not wanted to listen. Now I remember, the night before last – it was Bertha's birthday. It was between two and three in the morning and I sat up reading. You screamed as if someone was suffocating you: 'Get back! Get back!' I thumped on the wall because – I didn't want to hear any more. I've long had my suspicions, but I didn't dare to hear them confirmed. This is how I have suffered for you, what can you do for me?

LAURA: What can I do! I can swear before God and all that's sacred that you are Bertha's father.

CAPTAIN: What use is that, when you have said before that a mother can and should commit any crime for her children's sake. I beg you, for the sake of our memories together, I beg you as one wounded begs for the merciful death blow: tell me all. Don't you see that I am helpless as a child, don't you hear I'm appealing to you, like a child to its mother, don't you want to forget that I am a man, a soldier, who with one word can tame man and beast; I ask only for sympathy like an invalid, I take down my colours and call for mercy for my life.

LAURA: (*Approaches him and puts her hand on his brow.*) What! You're crying, man!

CAPTAIN: Yes, I am crying, though I am a man. But hasn't a man eyes? Hasn't a man hands, limbs, senses, thoughts, passions? Doesn't he live by the same nourishment, isn't he wounded by the same weapons, isn't he warmed and frozen by the same winter and summer as a woman? If you prick us, do we not bleed? If you tickle us, do we not laugh? If you poison us, do not die? Why shouldn't a man complain, or a soldier cry? Because it's unmanly! Why is it unmanly?

LAURA: Go on cry my child, Mama is here again. Do you remember that it was as a second mother that I first entered your life? Your big strong body was weak, you were a giant baby, which had either come too soon into the world or was perhaps unwanted.

CAPTAIN: Yes, I suppose that is how it was; Father and mother didn't want me and so I was born without a will. That's why it seemed to me, I made myself whole when you and I became one, and that's why I let you rule; I became, I, who in the barrack room, in front of the company was the commander, with you I became the one to obey, and I grew used to you, grew up at your side, looked up to you as a more gifted being, listened to you as if I was your foolish child.

LAURA: Yes, that's how it was then, and so I loved you like a child. But then, and I suppose you saw it, every time your feelings changed their nature and you approached me as my lover, I became shy and your embraces were to me a joy, that were followed by pangs of conscience as if my blood was ashamed. A mother who had become the lover, ugh!

CAPTAIN: I saw it, but I didn't understand it. And when I thought I could detect contempt of my unmanliness I wanted to conquer you as a woman by being a man.

LAURA: Yes, and that was your mistake. The mother was your friend, you see, but the woman is your enemy, and love between the sexes is a battle; and don't think I gave myself; I didn't give myself, rather I took – what I wanted. But you had the advantage, which I felt and which I wanted you to feel.

CAPTAIN: You always had the advantage; you could hypnotise me, so that I neither saw nor heard, just obeyed; you could give me a raw potato and convince me it was a peach; you could force me to admire your idiotic fancies as strokes of genius; you could have driven me to crime, to despicable acts. For you lacked sense, and instead of following my advice, you followed your own mind. But later, when I woke up and began to reflect, I felt that my honour was infringed, I wanted to blot it out by means of a great act, an achievement or discovery or an honourable suicide. I wanted to go to war, but wasn't allowed. That's when I threw myself into science. Now, when I was about to stretch out my hand to take the fruits of my labours, you cut off my arm. Now I am without honour and can't go on living, for a man can't live without honour.

LAURA: But a woman?

CAPTAIN: Yes, for she has her children, but he hasn't. – But we, and other men and women, have lived our lives as unaware as children, full of fantasies, ideals and delusions, and then we woke up; it was all right, but we woke with our feet on the pillow, and the one who woke us up was also a sleepwalker. When women get old and stop being women, they get beards on their chins, I wonder what men get, when they are old and have stopped being men? Those who sounded cock crow, no longer cocks but capons, and the hens answered the false call, so that when the sun should have risen, we found ourselves sitting in the light of the full moon amongst the ruins, just like in the good old days. We'd only been dozing having wild dreams, and there was no awakening.

LAURA: You should have been a writer, you know!

CAPTAIN: Who knows!

LAURA: I'm sleepy now, if you have any more fantasies, save them till tomorrow.

CAPTAIN: First one word more about reality. Do you hate me?

LAURA: Yes, sometimes! When you are a man.

CAPTAIN: That's like race hatred. If it is true that we descend from the apes, it must at least have been from two species. We are not alike are we, you and I?

LAURA: What are you trying to say?

CAPTAIN: I feel that in the struggle one of us must perish.

LAURA: Which?

CAPTAIN: The weakest naturally!

LAURA: And the stronger is in the right?

CAPTAIN: Always in the right, since he holds the power!

LAURA: Then I am right.

CAPTAIN: Do you already hold the power then?

LAURA: Yes, and legal power at that, when I have you certified tomorrow.

CAPTAIN: Certified?

LAURA: Yes! And then I'll bring up my child myself without listening to your visions.

CAPTAIN: And who will pay for the upbringing when I am no longer here?

LAURA: Your pension!

CAPTAIN: (*Approaches her threateningly.*) How can you have me certified?

LAURA: (*Takes out a letter.*) With this letter, an attested copy of which has been lodged with the authorities.

CAPTAIN: What letter?

LAURA: (*Withdraws towards the door left.*) Yours! Your statement to the doctor that you are mad!
(*The CAPTAIN looks at her dumbly.*)
You have fulfilled your purpose as an unfortunately necessary father and as a provider. You are no longer needed, and you must go. You must go since you have realised that my intelligence is just as strong as my will, and since you don't want to stay and admit it!
(*The CAPTAIN goes to table; picks up the lamp which is burning and throws it at LAURA, who has backed out through the doorway.*)

End of Act Two.

ACT THREE

Same set as before. But another lamp. The jib-door barricaded with a chair.

Scene 1

LAURA. The NURSE.

LAURA: Did he give you the keys?

NURSE: Give me them? No, God help me, but I took them out of the master's clothes which he had put out for Nöjd to brush.

CAPTAIN: So its Nöjd, who is on duty today.

NURSE: Yes, Nöjd himself!

CAPTAIN: Give me the keys!

NURSE: Yes, but it's plain stealing. Can you hear his footsteps up there. Backwards and forwards, backwards and forwards.

LAURA: Is the door locked?

NURSE: Oh yes, it's locked all right!

LAURA: (*Opens the bureau and sits at the desk top.*) Control your feelings, Margret, the best hope for all of us is to remain calm.
(*Knock on the door.*)
Who is it?

NURSE: (*Opens the door to the hall.*) It's Nöjd.

LAURA: Send him in!

NÖJD: (*Comes in.*) Despatch from the Colonel!

LAURA: Give it to me! (*Reads.*) So! – Nöjd, have you taken out all the cartridges, from the rifles and pouches?

NÖJD: As ordered!

LAURA: Wait out there until I've replied to the Colonel's letter!
(*NÖJD goes. LAURA writes.*)

NURSE: Listen madam! What's he up to up there!

LAURA: Quiet, I'm writing!
(*The sound of a saw.*)

67

NURSE: (*Half out loud to herself.*) Ah, merciful God help us! Where will it all end?

LAURA: There; give this to Nöjd! And my mother must know nothing about this! Do you hear!
(*The NURSE goes. LAURA opens drawer in the bureau and takes out papers.*)

Scene 2

LAURA. The PASTOR takes a chair and sits beside LAURA at the bureau.

PASTOR: Good evening, my dear sister. I've been away all day as you've heard and I've just got back. This is a sorry affair.

LAURA: Yes, brother, I've never known such a night and such a day.

PASTOR: Well, I can see you haven't come to any harm at all events.

LAURA: No, thank God, but imagine what could have happened.

PASTOR: But tell me one thing, how did it start. I've heard so many different stories.

LAURA: It started with his wild fantasy that he wasn't Bertha's father, and ended with him throwing a burning lamp in my face.

PASTOR: That's terrible! It's complete and utter madness. And what are we to do now?

LAURA: We must try to prevent further violence, and the Doctor has sent for a straitjacket from the hospital. Meanwhile I've sent a message to the Colonel to find out about the household's affairs, which he has managed in such a thoroughly reprehensible way.

PASTOR: What a deplorable business, but I've always expected something like it. Fire and water end up in an explosion! What've you got there in the drawer?

LAURA: (*Who has pulled out a drawer from the bureau.*) Look, this is where he's hidden everything!

PASTOR: (*Rummages in the drawer.*) My God! Here is your
doll; and your baptismal bonnet; and Bertha's rattle; and
your letters; and that locket... (*Dries his eyes.*)
He must have been very much in love with you, anyway,
Laura. I don't keep anything like that!

LAURA: I think he used to love me once, but time, time
changes so much!

PASTOR: What's that big paper? – A receipt for a grave! –
Yes, rather the grave than the asylum! Laura! Tell me:
aren't you at all to blame in this?

LAURA: Me? In what way am I supposed to be to blame
for a person going insane?

PASTOR: All right, I'm not saying anything! Blood is
thicker than water after all!

LAURA: What do you take the liberty of meaning by that?

PASTOR: (*Looks at her.*) Listen to me now!

LAURA: What?

PASTOR: Listen! You can't very well deny that it corresponds
to your wishes that you bring up your child by yourself.

LAURA: I don't understand!

PASTOR: How I admire you!

LAURA: Me! Mm!

PASTOR: And I'm to be the steward of that freethinker's
affairs! You know, I've always considered him a weed in
our pasture!

LAURA: (*A short suppressed laugh; then suddenly serious.*) You
dare to say that to me his wife?

PASTOR: You are too strong for me, Laura! Incredibly
strong! Like a fox in a trap: you'd rather cut off your
own leg than allow yourself to be caught! – Like a master
thief: no accomplice, not even your own conscience! –
Look at yourself in the mirror! You don't dare!

LAURA: I never use mirrors!

PASTOR: No, you daren't! – Can I see your hand! – No
bloodstain to betray you, no trace of the insidious poison!
An innocent little murder, not punishable by law; an
unconscious crime; unconscious? That's a fine discovery!
Do you hear him working away up there! – Beware; if
that man gets free, he'll cut you into little pieces!

LAURA: You talk too much, as if you had a bad conscience!
– Accuse me; if you can!

PASTOR: I can't!

LAURA: You see! You can't, and therefore I am innocent! –
You take care of your ward and I'll take care of mine! –
There's the Doctor!

Scene 3

As before. The DOCTOR.

LAURA: (*Rises.*) Welcome, Doctor. You will help me at least.
Won't you? And there's nothing much to be done here
unfortunately. Do you hear him, pacing about up there?
Are you convinced now?

DOCTOR: I'm convinced that an act of violence has been
committed, but now the question is, if that act of
violence was an outbreak of rage or of insanity!

PASTOR: But apart from the outburst you must admit he
has fixed ideas.

DOCTOR: I think, Pastor, that your ideas are more fixed
than his!

PASTOR: My firm opinions on matters of the highest...

DOCTOR: We'll leave opinions for now! – Madam, it is up
to you if you want to have your husband found guilty
and sent to prison or fined or have him sent to hospital!
What do you think of the Captain's behaviour?

LAURA: I can't answer that now!

DOCTOR: You don't have any firm opinions regarding
what is in the best interests of the family? What do you
say Pastor?

PASTOR: Yes, there will be a scandal either way...it's hard
to say.

LAURA: But if he is only fined for his violence, then he
may repeat it.

DOCTOR: And if he is sent to prison he'll soon be released.
So we consider it then in the best interests of all parties
that he is immediately treated as insane. – Where's the
nurse?

LAURA: What?

DOCTOR: She must put the straitjacket on the patient, when I've spoken to him and given the word! But not before! I have – the garment outside! (*Goes out to the hall and comes back with a large package.*) Be so good as to ask the nurse to come in!

(*LAURA rings.*)

PASTOR· Dreadful, dreadful!

(*The NURSE comes in.*)

DOCTOR: (*Takes out the straitjacket.*) Look here now! The idea is that you sneak this straitjacket up on the Captain from behind, when I deem it necessary, to prevent violent outbursts. As you see it has unusually long sleeves, that is in order to restrict his movements. And you tie them up at the back. Here are two straps that go through these buckles, which you then fasten to the arm of the chair or the sofa as is convenient. Will you do that?

NURSE: No, Doctor, I can't do that, I can't.

LAURA: Why don't you do it yourself, Doctor?

DOCTOR: Because the patient mistrusts me. It's really most appropriate that you do it, but I fear he mistrusts you too.

(*LAURA pulls a face.*)

Perhaps you Pastor...

PASTOR: No, I must decline!

Scene 4

As before. NÖJD.

LAURA: Have you already sent the despatch?

NÖJD: As ordered!

DOCTOR: So it's you, Nöjd! You know the circumstances and that the Captain is mentally ill. You must help us to take care of the patient.

NÖJD: If I can do anything for the Captain, he knows I'll do it!

DOCTOR: You are to put this straitjacket on him...

NURSE: No, he mustn't touch him; Nöjd mustn't hurt him. Then I'd rather do it, gently, gently! But Nöjd you can stand outside and come and help me, if it's necessary... yes, that's what you must do. (*A banging on the door.*)

DOCTOR: He's there! Put the straitjacket under your shawl on the chair, and everyone go out for now, the Pastor and I will receive him, because that door won't hold for very long. – Out you go, now!

NURSE: (*Goes out left.*) Lord Jesus help us!
(*LAURA closes the bureau; then goes out left. NÖJD goes out, upstage.*)

Scene 5

The jib-door bursts open the chair is sent across the floor and the lock breaks. The CAPTAIN comes out with a pile of books under his arm. The DOCTOR and the PASTOR.

CAPTAIN: (*Puts the books on the table.*) Here it all is, in all these books. So I wasn't mad. It says here in the *Odyssey* Book One line 215 page six in the Upsala translation. Telemachus is speaking to Athene. 'My mother claims that he, whom they call Odysseus, is my father; but for myself I don't know, for no man yet knew his origins.' And this suspicion is harboured by Telemachus about Penelope, the most virtuous of women. That's fine, isn't it! Eh! Here is the prophet Ezekiel: 'The fool saith; see here is my father, but who can tell whose loins have begotten him.'

That's clear! What's this? Merzläkov's history of Russian Literature. 'Alexander Pushkin, Russia's great bard, sent to his death more by the widespread rumours of his wife's unfaithfulness than by the bullet in his breast received in a duel. On his deathbed he swore she was innocent.' Ass! ass! How could he swear to that? You can see in any case that I'm reading my books! – Hello, Jonas, are you here! And the Doctor, of course! Have you heard what I answered an English lady, who

complained that Irishmen throw lighted lamps in their
wives' faces? – My God, those women, I said! – Women?
she lisped! – Yes, naturally! I replied. When it gets to the
point where a man, a man who has loved and adored a
woman, goes and takes a burning lamp and slams it in
her face, that's when you know?!

PASTOR: Know what?

CAPTAIN: Nothing! You never know anything, you just
believe, isn't that true, Jonas? You believe and you are
blessed. Yes, but I know you can be damned by your
faith! I know that!

DOCTOR: Captain!

CAPTAIN: Quiet! I don't want to talk to you; I don't want
to hear you relaying like a telephone what they're saying
in there! In there! You know! – So Jonas, do you think
you are the father of your children? I remember you had
a tutor at home, who was pretty under the eyebrows and
whom people used to talk about.

PASTOR: Adolf! – Take care!

CAPTAIN: Lift up your wig, and see if there aren't a couple
of lumps there. My God I think he's gone pale! Yes-yes,
it's only talk, but my God, they talk so much. But we're
all of us absurd wretches we married men. Isn't that true,
Doctor? Now how did it go with your marriage couch?
Wasn't there a lieutenant in your house, eh? Wait let me
guess? His name was... – (*Whispers in the DOCTOR's ear.*)
– You see, he's gone pale too! Don't be upset. She's dead
and buried, and what's done can't be done again! I knew
him actually and now he's a – – – look at me Doctor! –
No, in the eyes – a major in the Dragoons! By God I swear
if he hasn't sprouted horns as well!

DOCTOR: (*Troubled.*) Captain, can we talk about
something else?

CAPTAIN: You see! He at once wants to talk about
something else when I want to talk about horns!

PASTOR: You know brother, that you are mentally ill.

CAPTAIN: Yes, I know very well. But if you let me take
care of your crowned heads a little while, I'd soon be

locking you up too! I am mad, but how did I become so? It doesn't concern you and it doesn't concern anyone! Would you like to talk about something else now. (*Picks up the photo album from the table.*) Lord Jesus, that's my child! Mine? We can't know that of course? Do you know what we must do, to be able to know that? First we get married in order to be socially respectable; then you separate soon after; and become lovers; and adopt the children. Then at least you can be sure they are your own adoptive children? That's right, isn't it? But what does all that help me now? What can help me, now that you've taken my idea of eternity away from me, what does science and philosophy gain, when I have nothing to live for, what can I do with life, when I have no honour? I grafted my right arm, half my brain, half my spinal cord on to another stem, because I thought they would grow together and entwine themselves into one single more complete tree, and then along comes someone with a knife and cuts away below the graft, and then I am just half a tree, but the other one keeps growing with my arm, half my brain, whilst I wither and die, for they were the best parts that I gave away. Now I want to die! Do with me what you will! I don't exist any more: (*The DOCTOR whispers with the PASTOR; they go into the apartment left; a few moments later BERTHA comes out.*)

Scene 6

The CAPTAIN. BERTHA. The CAPTAIN sits collapsed by the table.

BERTHA: (*Goes to him.*) Are you ill, Papa?

CAPTAIN: (*Looks up listlessly.*) Me?

BERTHA: Do you know what you have done? Do you know you threw the lamp at mother?

CAPTAIN: Did I?

BERTHA: Yes, you did! Imagine if she had been hurt?

CAPTAIN: What would that have mattered?

BERTHA: You're not my father, if you can speak like that!

CAPTAIN: What did you say? Am I not your father? How
do you know? Who told you so? And who is your father
then? Who?

BERTHA: Well not you, anyway!

CAPTAIN: Still not me! Who then? Who? You seem to be
well informed! Who's informed you? Must I endure that
my child looks me in the eye and tells me I am not her
father! Don't you know that is an insult to your mother?
Don't you understand that it is to her shame if that is so?

BERTHA: Don't say anything about Mama, do you hear!

CAPTAIN: No, you're all sticking together, all of you
against me! And that's how it's been all along!

BERTHA: Papa!

CAPTAIN: Don't use that word again!

BERTHA: Papa, Papa!

CAPTAIN: (*Pulls her to him.*) Bertha, dear beloved child,
of course you are my child! Yes, yes; it can't be any
other way. It is so! All that was just morbid thoughts,
that came with the wind like plague and fevers. Look at
me, let me see my soul in your eyes! – But I can see her
soul too! You have two souls, and you love me with one
and hate me with the other. But you shall love only me!
You shall have only one soul, or you'll never be in peace,
and neither shall I. You shall have one thought only,
which is the offspring of my own thought, you shall have
only one will, and that shall be mine.

BERTHA: I don't want to! I want to be myself.

CAPTAIN: You can't. You see, I'm a cannibal and I want to
eat you. Your mother wants to eat me but I didn't let her.
I am Saturn, who ate his children because he had foreseen
that they would eat him otherwise. To eat or be eaten!
That is the question! If I don't eat you, you'll eat me, and
you've already shown me your teeth! But don't be afraid,
my beloved child, I won't harm you! (*Goes to the weapons
case and takes a revolver.*)

BERTHA: (*Tries to escape.*) Help, Mama, help, he's going to
murder me!

NURSE: (*Comes in.*) Mr Adolf, what is it?

CAPTAIN: (*Examines the revolver.*) Have you taken the cartridges?

NURSE: Well, I have tidied them away, but sit down here and be calm, and I'll go and get them!
(*She leads the CAPTAIN by the arm to the chair, where he sits listlessly. Whereupon she takes out the straitjacket and stands behind the chair. BERTHA sneaks out left.*)
Mr Adolf, do your remember, when you were my darling little boy, and I tucked you up at night, and said your prayers with you. And do you remember when I'd get up in the night and bring you a drink; remember how I'd light the candles and tell you lovely stories, when you had bad dreams and couldn't sleep. Remember?

CAPTAIN: Say more, Margret, it calms my head so well! Tell me more!

NURSE: All right, but you must listen then! Do you remember the time you took the big kitchen knife and wanted to carve boats and I came in and had to coax the knife away from you. You were a silly child and I had to trick you, because you didn't believe that it was for your own good. – Give me that snake, I said, or otherwise he'll bite! And then you gave me the knife! (*She takes the revolver from him.*) And then when you had to get dressed and didn't want to. I had to coax you and say you'd get a gold coat and be dressed as a prince. And then I took the little waistcoat, which was just made of green wool, and held it in front of you and said: pop in both your arms! and then I said: sit there nice and quietly, while I do up the buttons behind! (*She has put the straitjacket on him.*) And then I said: get up now and walk nicely across the floor, so I can see if it fits... (*She leads him to the sofa.*) And then I said: now you must lie down and go to sleep.

CAPTAIN: What did you say? Am I to go to bed with my clothes on! – Damnation! What've you done to me! (*Tries to get loose.*) Ah, damn you, cunning woman! Who'd imagine you'd have the brains! (*He lies on the sofa.*) Imprisoned, done for, outwitted, and unable to die!

NURSE: Forgive me Adolf, forgive me, but I wanted to stop you killing the child!

CAPTAIN: Why didn't you let me kill the child? Life is
hell and death is heaven, and children belong in heaven!

NURSE: What do you know about what comes after death?

CAPTAIN: That's all one does know, but about life one
knows nothing! Oh, if only one had known from the
beginning.

NURSE: Mr Adolf! Humble your hard heart and appeal to
God for mercy, it's still not too late. It wasn't too late
for the thief on the cross, when the Saviour said: today
you will be with me in paradise!

CAPTAIN: Crowing for corpses already, you old crow!
(*The NURSE takes a psalm book out of her pocket.*)
(*Calls.*) Nöjd! Is Nöjd there!
(*NÖJD comes in.*)
Throw that woman out! She'll kill us all with her psalms.
Throw her out the window or up the chimney or whatever.

NÖJD: (*Looks at the NURSE.*) God keep you Captain, but,
but I can't! I just can't! Six men, yes, but a woman!

CAPTAIN: Can't handle a woman, eh?

NÖJD: I can handle a woman, but it's just that there's
something odd about raising your hand to a woman.

CAPTAIN: What's odd about it? Haven't they raised their
hands against me?

NÖJD: Yes, but I can't, Captain! It's just as if you were to
ask me to hit the Pastor. It's like religion, it's in the
blood! I can't!

Scene 7

As before. LAURA gestures to NÖJD to go.

CAPTAIN: Omphale! Omphale! Playing with the cudgel,
while Hercules spins your wool!

LAURA: (*Goes over to the sofa.*) Adolf! Look at me. Do you
think I am your enemy?

CAPTAIN: Yes I do. I think you are all my enemies!
My mother, who didn't want to bring me into the world,
because my birth would be painful, was my enemy, when

77

she deprived the embryo of nourishment and made a half cripple out of me! My sister was my enemy, when she taught me subservience to her. The first woman I embraced was my enemy, when she gave me ten years of illness in repayment for the love I gave her. My daughter became my enemy, when she had to choose between you and me. And you, my wife, you were my deadly enemy, for you wouldn't leave me alone, until I was left lifeless!

LAURA: I don't know if I've thought or intended, what you accuse me of. It can happen that a vague desire to get rid of you like a hindrance was aroused in me, but if you detect any plan in my conduct, then it's possible it was there, although I didn't see it. I've never reflected over the events, rather they have glided forwards on rails, that you have laid down yourself, and before God and my own conscience, I feel innocent even if I am not. Your existence has been for me like a stone on my heart, which has pressed and pressed until my heart had to shake off the oppressive weight. That's how it is I'm sure, and if I have unwittingly hurt you, then I ask your forgiveness.

CAPTAIN: That sounds plausible! But what does that help me? And whose is the fault? It is the fault of marriage perhaps? Before one married a wife; now you enter into business partnership with a woman pursuing her career, or you move in with a friend! – And so you bed your partner, and violate your friend! What happened to love, healthy sensual love? Well that died in the attempt! And what of the progeny of this stocks and shares love made payable to the bearer, with limited liability? Who is the stockholder when the crash comes? Who is the corporal father to the spiritual child?

LAURA: And as for your suspicions about the child, they are altogether unfounded.

CAPTAIN: That's the terrible thing! If they were at least well founded, then there would be something to get hold of, something to cling to. Now there are only shadows, hiding in the bushes and sticking their heads out laughing, it's like punching the air, fighting mock battles with blanks. A fatal reality would have provoked resistance, spurred my life and soul into action, but now...my thoughts dissolve into evaporation, and my brain ticks over until it catches fire! Give me a pillow under my head! And put something over me, I'm cold! I'm so terribly cold!

(*LAURA takes her shawl and spreads it over him. The NURSE goes out for a pillow.*)

LAURA: Give me your hand, friend!

CAPTAIN: My hand! That you have tied behind my back... Omphale! Omphale! But I feel your soft shawl against my lips; it's so warm and so soft like your arm, and it smells of vanilla like your hair did when you were young! Laura, when you were young, and we went out in the birch wood with primroses and thrushes, so lovely, lovely. Think how wonderful life has been and what has become of it. You didn't want it to become like this, neither did I, and it happened anyway. Who has any power over life!

LAURA: God alone...

CAPTAIN: The God of battle then! Or Goddess as it now seems! Get this cat off me! Take it away!

(*The NURSE returns with a pillow, takes away the shawl.*)

Give me my tunic! – Throw it over me!

(*The NURSE takes the tunic from the hanger and puts it over him.*)

Oh my bold lion skin that you wanted to take from me. Omphale! Omphale! You cunning woman, friend of peace, who discovered how to disarm. Wake up Hercules, before they take the cudgel away from you! You'd lure us out of our armour too, telling us it's tinsel. But it was iron, before it was tinsel. It used to be the smith, who made my tunics, but now it's the embroiderer! Omphale! Omphale! Raw strength has fallen before insidious weakness, to hell with you, cursed women and damn your sex! (*He pulls himself up to spit but falls back on to the sofa.*) What kind of a pillow have you given me, Margret! It's so hard and cold, so cold! Come and sit here beside me on the chair. That's it! Can I put my head in your lap! There! – That's warmer! Lean over me so that I can feel your breast. Oh, it's sweet to fall asleep at a woman's breast, be it the mother's or the lover's, but the sweetest is the mother's!

LAURA: Do you wish to see your child, Adolf? Tell me!

CAPTAIN: My child? A man has no children, it's only women who have children, and therefore the future is theirs while we die childless! – Oh, gentle Jesus meek and mild, look upon this little child!

NURSE: Listen, he's praying to God!

CAPTAIN: No, to you, I'm asking you to send me to sleep because I'm tired, so tired! Good night Margret, and blessed be thou amongst women! (*He raises himself, but falls down with a cry into the NURSE's lap.*)

Scene 8

LAURA goes left and calls the DOCTOR who comes out with the PASTOR.

LAURA: Help us, Doctor, if it's not too late! Look, he's stopped breathing!

DOCTOR: (*Examines patient's pulse.*) It's a stroke!

PASTOR: Is he dead?

DOCTOR: No, he could still revive, but what kind of recovery it would be I don't know.

PASTOR: After death comes judgement...

DOCTOR: No judgement! And no accusations! You, who believe that God controls human destinies, will have to talk to him about this affair.

NURSE: Oh, Pastor, he prayed to God in his last moments!

PASTOR: (*To LAURA.*) Is it true?

LAURA: It's true!

DOCTOR: In that case, of which I can no more be the judge than I can the cause of this malady, my work ends here. Yours begins, Pastor.

LAURA: Is that all you've got to say at his deathbed, Doctor?

DOCTOR: That's all! I know no more. Whoever knows more, let him speak!

BERTHA: (*Comes in from left and runs to her mother.*) Mama, Mama!

LAURA: My child! My own child!

PASTOR: Amen!

The End

MISS JULIE

Fröken Julie

a naturalistic tragedy

(1888)

INTRODUCTION

August Strindberg

Theatre has long seemed to me, like the fine arts in general, to be a *Biblia Pauperum*, a bible with pictures for those who cannot read the written or printed word, and the theatre writer to be a lay preacher distributing the current thinking in popular form, so popular that the middle classes, who in the main frequent the theatres, can without too much mental strain, understand what the main issue is. Theatre has therefore always been an elementary school for youths, the half educated, and women, who still retain the lower capacity to deceive themselves and allow themselves to be deceived, that is to say to have delusions, to receive the suggestions of the writer. It has seemed to me therefore that in our time, when the rudimentary, incomplete thinking which occurs in the imagination has appeared to develop into reflection, examination and testing, that theatre, like religion, was well on the way to being laid to rest as a dying form for the enjoyment of which there lacks the requisite conditions. That this assumption might be true is indicated by the total crisis in the theatre which is affecting the whole of Europe, and not least by the fact that in the great cultural nations, which have long produced the greatest thinkers, namely England and Germany, theatre is dead, along with for the most part the other fine arts.

In other countries it has been thought possible to create a new drama by filling the old forms with the contents of a newer age; to start with, the new thinkers haven't yet had time to be popularised so that the public can have the sense to know what is at issue, and then the warring parties have stirred up people's minds, so that there is no place for a pure interested enjoyment, for one is contradicted to one's core, and a clapping and whistling majority has exercised its oppression in that very public way that it can in a theatre, and then too the new form for the new content is still lacking, so that the new wine is splitting the old skins.

In previous plays I haven't attempted anything new – for one cannot – except only to modernise the form according to the requirements which I imagined the new people of today would have upon this art form. And to that end I have chosen, or allowed myself to be seized by, a motif which could be said to lay outside the contemporary party struggle, while the questions of social elevation or demotion, higher or lower, better or worse, man or woman, are, have been and shall be, of abiding interest. When I took this motif from life, an incident I heard talked about a number of years ago when the event made a strong impression upon me, I found it suitable for a tragedy, for it still gives a tragic impression to see a fortunate individual go under, even more to see a family die out. But there will come a time perhaps when we have become so developed, so enlightened, that we can look with indifference upon the crude, cynical, heartless drama that life presents us, when we have discarded these inferior unreliable engines of thought that we call feelings, which will have become superfluous and harmful, when our facility for judgement has reached maturity. When the heroine arouses our sympathy it is only because of our weakness in not being able to resist the feeling of fear that the fate could befall us. However, the very sensitive audience should still not be satisfied with this sympathy. All the men of the future with faith can perhaps supply some positive suggestions to stave off evil, a bit of policy, in other words. But to begin with, there is no absolute evil, for one family's downfall is of course a benefit for another family that may rise, and the alternation of rising and falling supplies one of life's greatest pleasures, when happiness lies only in comparison. And of the policy which will stave off the sorry condition in which the bird of prey eats the dove and the louse eats the bird of prey I would like to ask: why should it be prevented? Life isn't so mathematic-idiotic that the great eat the small, but rather it happens just as often that the bee will kill the lion, or at least drive it mad.

That my tragedy gives a tragic impression to many is the fault of the many. When we become strong like the first French revolutionaries it will give an unmitigated good and happy impression to behold the royal oaks pruned of their decayed and superannuated trees which have stood too long in the way of others with just as much right to flourish for their time, a good impression as when one sees the incurably sick at last allowed to die.

My tragedy *The Father* was recently reproached for being tragic as if what one has demanded was jolly plays. One spoke pretentiously of the joy of life and theatre managers commissioned farces as if the joy of life lay in being ridiculous and depicting people as if they were all struck down with St Vitus' dance or idioticism. I find the joy of life in life's powerful grim struggles, and my enjoyment lies in being able to know something, able to learn something. And therefore I have chosen an unusual case, but an instructive one, an exception in a word but an important exception that proves the rule, which will probably offend those who love the banal. What shall further dismay the simple mind is that my motivation of the action is not simple, and that the point of view is not a single one. An event in real life – and this is a rather new discovery – is produced usually by a whole series of more or less deep-lying motives, but the audience chooses for the most part that which is for his mind the most easily understood or which does most credit to his judgement. Here is a suicide, a bad business – says the citizen – Unhappy love! say the ladies – Physical illness! say the sick – Crushed hopes! say the shipwrecked. But it could be that the motive lay elsewhere, or nowhere, and the fact that the departed hid the basic motive by presenting a wholly different one does more credit to his memory.

I have motivated Miss Julie's tragic fate with a whole load of circumstances; the mother's basic instincts; the father's incorrect upbringing of the girl; her own character and the fiancé's suggestions imposed upon her weak degenerated mind; furthermore the party atmosphere of midsummer eve; the absence of her father, her period, her association with the animals; the arousing influence of the dance; the effect of the twilight; the strong aphrodisiac effect of the flowers; and finally chance which throws the two together in a secluded place, plus the aroused man's attraction to her.

I have tried, not to proceed exclusively physiologically, neither monomaniacally psychologically, not only blamed heredity from the mother, nor thrown all the blame on her period nor exclusively upon 'immorality', I have not only preached morals. This last I have left to the cook for want of a priest.

With this multiplicity of causes I must applaud myself for being in keeping with the times! And if others have done it before me, I applaud myself for not being alone with my paradoxes, as all discoveries are called.

As far as character descriptions are concerned I have made the figures of this drama rather characterless for the following reasons:

The word 'character' has over the years acquired many meanings. It originally meant the dominant basic feature of the mind complex and was confused with temperament. Then it became the middle-class expression for the machine; so that an individual who once and for all has stopped at his natural point or adapted himself to a certain role in life, stopped growing in other words, came to be called a character, and he who was in a stage of development, the skilful navigator on the river of life, who doesn't sail with a fixed sail but rather raises the sail to turn into the wind is called 'characterless'. In the derogatory sense, naturally, since he is so difficult to capture, categorise and keep track of. This bourgeois concept of the unchanging nature of the soul is transferred to the stage, where the bourgeois has always dominated. A character there is a gentleman who is fixed and complete, who unchangingly appears drunk, jovial, pitiful, and whom to characterise there needs only physical deformity, a club foot, a wooden leg, a red nose, or to have the person concerned repeat a phrase such as 'how gallant!' or 'Barkis is willing' and so on. This simplified way of seeing people remains even in the great Molière. Harpagon is simply miserly even if he manages to be both miserly and a good financier, a splendid father, a good citizen and, what is worse, his 'deformity' is extremely advantageous for his son-in-law and daughter who inherit his wealth and therefore shouldn't criticise him even though they can wait a little to climb into bed. I don't believe therefore in simple characters, and the writers' summary judgements over people; he is stupid, he is a brute, this one is jealous, that one is mean and so on ought to be challenged by naturalistic writers, who know how rich the human soul is and who sense that vice has a reverse side which closely resembles virtue.

As modern characters living in a transitional period, more hasty and hysterical at least than previous times, I have drawn my figures more vacillating, shattered, composed of both old and new, and it doesn't seem to me unlikely that modern ideas by means of newspapers and conversation have trickled down to the level where servants live.

My characters are agglomerations of bygone and contemporary culture, bits from books and papers, fragments of people, shreds of Sunday clothes turned rags, in quite the same way as the soul is patched together. I have also provided documentation of character development, when I allow the weaker character to steal and repeat the words of the stronger, and let characters borrow ideas, or suggestions as they call it, from each other.

Miss Julie is a modern character, not that the half-woman man-hater hasn't existed in all periods but because it is now she has been discovered, has stepped forwards and made a lot of noise. The half-woman is a type who pushes herself forwards nowadays selling herself for power, honours, decorations, diplomas, as they did for money before. She is corrupt. They are a poor species, don't last but unfortunately propagate themselves by the wretchedness they cause; degenerate men seem to unconsciously choose their mates from among them so that they reproduce offspring, of undecided gender for whom life is a torture but who unfortunately perish either in disharmony with reality or through uncontrolled outbreaks of their repressed instincts or through the disappointment of their hopes of achieving equality with men. It is a tragic type, providing the spectacle of a struggle against nature; tragic as a romantic heritage squandered by naturalism, which only wants happiness; but happiness is the preserve of a good and strong species.

But Miss Julie is also a leftover from the old military aristocracy which is now giving way to the new neurotic or intellectual nobility; a victim of the disharmonies a mother's 'transgression' has introduced into the family; a victim of the mistaken notions of the age, of circumstances, her own flawed constitution, which altogether add up to the old idea of destiny or universal law. The Naturalist has eradicated guilt with God, but the consequences of actions, punishment, prison or the fear of it he cannot remove for the simple reason that they remain, acquittal or no. For those fellow-beings wronged against cannot be so indulgent on those outsiders who are not wronged against, and they cannot afford to be. Even if the father was impelled to postpone the revenge the daughter would take revenge upon herself, as she does here driven by the innate or acquired sense of horror the upper classes inherit – from where? From barbarism, from their Aryan forefathers, medieval chivalry which is very beautiful but these days not conducive to the survival of the species. It is the nobleman's *harikiri*, the Japanese law of conscience which tells him to slit open his stomach when another insults him and which survives in modified form in the duel, the privilege of the nobility. Thus the servant survives, but Miss Julie cannot live without honour. The slave has the advantage over the knight – that he lacks his fatal preoccupation with honour. But in all us Aryans there is a trace of the knight or Don Quixote which makes us sympathise with the suicide who has done a dishonourable deed and so lost his honour and we are sufficiently noblemen to be embarrassed to see fallen greatness lying like a discarded corpse. Yes, even if the fallen should stand up again and atone through honourable actions. The servant Jean is the type who founds a line, in him we see differentiation. The son of a poor peasant, he has educated himself so he is a potential gentleman. He is a quick learner, his finely tuned sense (smell, taste, sight) and an eye for beauty. He already has risen in the world and is strong enough not to mind standing on someone else's shoulders. He is already a stranger in his own environment which he despises as a world he has left behind him; he fears the people and flees them since they know his secrets, divine his intentions and enviously watch his ascension, and gleefully his fall. From this comes his double, indeterminate nature, vacillating between sympathy for the upper classes and hate for those who constitute it. He calls himself an aristocrat, has made himself privy to its secrets, is polished but raw underneath, already wears a tailcoat tastefully but offers no guarantees of a clear body beneath it.

He respects Miss Julie but is afraid of Kristin since she knows his dangerous secrets; he is sufficiently insensitive not to allow the night's events to interfere with his plans for the future. With the roughness of a slave and the master's lack of squeamishness, he can see blood without swooning, shrug off misfortune. For this reason he will leave the fray unharmed and probably end up as a hotelier, and if he doesn't become a Romanian count, then his son will probably become a student and a barrister.

Besides this, the information he gives is about the lower classes view of life, seen from below, is important, that is when he is telling the truth, which he doesn't often do, for he says more what is advantageous for him than what is true. When Miss Julie throws out the suggestion that all those in the lower classes feel sorely the oppression from above, Jean naturally agrees, since he wants her sympathy, but he soon corrects himself when he sees the advantage of distinguishing himself from the masses.

Apart from the fact that he is in the ascendant, he has the advantage over Miss Julie in that he is a man. In terms of gender he is the aristocrat by virtue of his masculine strength, his more finely developed senses and his ability to take the initiative – his inferiority is mostly in this temporary social environment in which he lives and which he probably puts aside along with his jacket.

His slave mentality expresses itself in his respect for the Count (the boots) and his religious superstition; but he respects the count rather as the holder of the superior position, which he himself aims at; and that respect remains after he has made a conquest of the daughter and seen how worthless the beautiful shell really is.

I do not think any love relationship in any higher meaning can exist between individuals of such dissimilar quality and therefore I have it that Miss Julie's feelings are fabricated as a defence or to protect her from guilt; Jean allows himself to presume he could love her if he could raise his social position. I think it is true since it is the same with love as with the hyacinth which has to put down roots in the darkness before it can produce a strong flower. Here it shoots it up and goes into bloom all at once and therefore the flower dies quickly.

Kristin, finally, is a female slave and lacking in independence. She is sluggish, bound to her stove and stuffed with morality and religion serving as blinkers and scapegoats. She goes to church to blithely shift her guilt for her petty thieving onto Jesus to get herself recharged of innocence. She is a supporting character and therefore deliberately sketched as I did with the priest and doctor in *The Father* since I only wanted everyday people, as country priest and provincial doctors are for the most part. If these characters seem abstract it is because ordinary people are to some degree abstract in the performance of their duties – conventional, only showing one side of themselves in their work, and so long as the spectator doesn't have the need to see them from several aspects, then my abstract stretch is reasonably true-to-life.

Finally, concerning the dialogue I have broken with tradition somewhat in that I don't have my characters sit and ask stupid questions in order to produce a witty riposte. I have avoided the symmetrical mathematical aspect of the style of dialogue and allowed their minds to function with irregularity as they do in reality where in a conversation no subject is ever fully exhausted but rather one brain finds in another a cog with which it can engage. Consequently the dialogue wanders about, providing itself with material in the opening scenes which is taken up later and developed, repeated, unfolded and added to, like themes in a musical composition.

The plot is tolerable enough, and since it really only concerns two people I have kept myself to these, only involving one minor character, the cook, and allowing the father's unhappy spirit to waft about above and behind it all. This is because I think, that the modern audience is mostly interested in the psychological events and our knowledge-hungry souls cannot be content to watch events before us without finding out the reason why. We want to see the strings, the machinery, examine the box with the false bottom, touch the magic ring to find the join, look at the cards to see how they are marked.

I have in this connection been mindful of the Goncourt brothers' realistic novels, which attract me the most of contemporary literature.

Concerning the technical aspects of the composition, I have tried removing the division into acts. This is because I thought that our diminishing suspension of disbelief could be disturbed by intervals, during which the audience have time to reflect and escape the writer-hypnotist's suggestive influence. My play lasts probably an hour and a half and since one can listen to a lecture or a sermon or a parliamentary debate lasting as long or longer, I allowed myself to imagine that a play wouldn't be tiresome if it lasted one and a half hours. Already in 1872 in one of my last theatrical efforts *The Outlaw* I tried this concentrated form though with little success. The piece was written in five acts and was finished, when I noticed its fragmentary, restless effect. I burned it and from the ashes emerged one long reworked act of fifty printed pages lasting one hour. The form is not entirely new but is considered to be my property but perhaps, thanks to the changes in public taste has the prospect of becoming appropriate to the age. My intention would ultimately be to train the public to be able to sit through a complete evening's entertainment in one act. But this requires research first. In the meantime, to provide rest points for the audience and the actors without releasing the audience from the illusion, I have used three art forms all belonging to the drama: the monologue, the mime and the ballet, originally part of the ancient tragedy, except that the monody is now a monologue, and the chorus is the ballet.

The monologue has now been banned by our realists as unlikely, but if I can motivate it and make it convincing then I can use it to advantage. It is believable that a speaker can talk and walk about alone in his room and read his speech aloud, likely that an actor goes over his role aloud, that a maid can talk to her cat, a mother prattle to her infant, an old maid chatter to her parrot, a sleeper talk in his sleep, and to allow the actor for once the chance to be free from the writer's control, it is better that the monologues be implied rather than specified. For since it matters little what one says in one's sleep, or to the parrot or the cat since it doesn't affect the action, then a talented actor attuned to the atmosphere and situation could possibly improvise it better than the writer, who cannot beforehand work out how much should be said or for how long before an audience will awaken from the illusion.

As is known, the Italian theatre has, in certain cases, returned to the improvisation, and in doing so created actors who write, albeit according to the writer's general plan, which can be an advantage or a nascent art form where one might say that art engenders art.

Where a monologue would seem unrealistic, I have used the mime and there I leave the actor even more liberty to create and gain credit independently. But so as not to be too demanding upon the audience I have allowed for music, though completely motivated by the midsummer dancing, to have its illusory sway over the dumb-show. Here the musical director should avoid, when choosing the pieces, not to evoke an inappropriate atmosphere by choosing pieces from currently popular operettas or dance tunes or too atmospheric folk tunes.

The ballet I have included cannot be replaced with a so-called crowd scene, which are always badly acted by a mob of idiots taking the opportunity to be clever and spoil the illusion.

Since the simple people here don't improvise their spiteful song but use ready-made material which has a double meaning, I have not written the song myself but taken a lesser-known song I have found myself in the Stockholm area. The words strike home broadly but not directly, but this is also the intention since the cunning (weakness) of the slave mentality is not the type to allow direct assault. So no talking clowns in what is anyway a serious piece of action, no crude sniggering over a situation which puts the lid on the family coffin.

As regards the decor I have borrowed from impressionist painting asymmetry and suggestion and in doing so I believe I have furthered the illusion: because not being able to see whole rooms allows space for the imagination to complete its own picture. I have also benefited by dispensing with tiresome exits through doors which are generally made of stage canvas and move about at the slightest touch, and lack even the capacity to allow an enraged father to leave the room after a bad dinner 'so that the whole house shakes' (in the theatre it waves). I have likewise confined myself to one set both to allow the characters to become one with their milieu and to get away from the habit of sumptuous sets. When there is only one set one can expect it to be lifelike – though nothing is more difficult than making a room like a room, however clever the painter can be at creating volcanoes spitting fire, and waterfalls. Let the walls be of canvas but it must be time to give up painting shelves and cooking utensils. We have so much else in the way of stage conventions that we are expected to believe in, that we might be excused having to believe in painted saucepans. I have placed the rear wall and the table at an angle so that the actors can face each other, at least in half profile, as they sit across the table from each other. At the opera *Aida* I saw the backcloth at an angle which led the eye off into an unknown perspective, and it didn't look as if it had been put that way simply out of boredom with straight lines.

Another perhaps not unnecessary innovation would be the removal of the footlights. This lighting is supposed to have the function of making the actors rounder in the face; but I should like to ask – why should all actors be round in the face? Doesn't this lighting eliminate many subtle expressions in the lower part of the face particularly the mouth, doesn't it falsify the shape of the nose and cast shadows up over the eyes? If this is not the case then one thing is certain; the pain caused to the actors' eyes so that any meaningful expression in them is lost, because the footlights strike the retina on parts which is normally protected (except among sailors who see the sun reflected in the water), and for this reason one rarely sees expressions in the eyes except crude staring, either to one side or up at the gallery so that we see the whites of their eyes. Perhaps we can also attribute to this the tiresome habit amongst actresses of fluttering their eyelashes. And when anyone on the stage wants to speak using their eyes, he has no alternative but to stare out straight into the audience which puts him into direct contact with them across the framework of the stage; this bad habit is known, rightly or wrongly, as 'greeting your friends'.

Wouldn't side lights of sufficient strength (using reflectors or some such) allow the actors to use their greatest resource to reinforce their mime – the expression of their eyes?

I have no great illusions of being able to get the actors to play for the audience rather than with it even though it would be desirable. I don't dream of being able to see an actor's back throughout a whole important scene, but I fervently wish that important scenes wouldn't be played in front of the prompter's box like duets, marked out for applause, but that they should be played in the appropriate place according to the situation. So, no revolutions, just small modifications, since to turn the stage into a room with the fourth wall missing, and with some of the furniture with its back to the audience would I suppose only be a distraction.

When I speak about make-up I cannot hope to be heard by the ladies who prefer beauty to truth. But the actor might well ponder if it is an advantage to him to apply an abstract character to his face which then sits there like a mark. Imagine a man who draws with soot a distinct angry expression between his eyes, and suppose that, with the permanently grim expression he has to deliver a line smiling. What a dreadful grimace that should be! And how is this false forehead, as smooth as a billiard ball, supposed to wrinkle when the old man gets really angry?

In a modern psychological drama where the subtlest motions of the soul are reflected upon the face rather by gestures and sound, it ought to be best to try strong sidelights on a small stage and with actors without make-up, or at least with a minimum of it.

If we could then dispense with the visible orchestra with the distracting lights on it and their faces turned to the audience; if we could raise the stalls to have the spectators sight-line above the actor's knees; if we could get rid of the boxes with their tittering diners and old ladies taking their supper, so that we could have complete darkness in the room during the performance; and first and foremost have a small stage and a small auditorium; then perhaps a new drama might emerge, a theatre once again at least a place for the entertainment and enlightenment of educated people. While we wait for such a theatre I suppose we shall have to write for storage and to build up the repertoire which must appear one day.

I have made an attempt; if I have failed then there's plenty of time to try again.

Characters

MISS JULIE
25 years

JEAN
servant, 30 years

KRISTIN
cook, 35 years

The Count's kitchen, midsummer eve.

A large kitchen, the ceiling and walls concealed by draperies and borders. The rear wall runs diagonally up from the left; on it, on the left are two shelves with copper, pewter, iron and tin utensils; the shelves lined with scalloped paper; a bit to the right three-quarters of the large arched outer doorway with two glass doors, through which can be seen a fountain with a statue of Cupid, lilac bushes in bloom and Lombardy poplars sticking up.

On the left of the stage the corner of a large tile stove, part of its hood showing. To the right, one end of the servants' kitchen table is sticking out, made of white pine, and some chairs. The stove is decorated with birch twigs; the floor is strewn with juniper. On the end of the table is a large Japanese spice jar with blooming lilacs. An icebox, a dresser and a sink. A large, old-fashioned servant bell above the door, a speaking tube emerges from the left side of the same.

KRISTIN stands by the stove frying in a frying-pan; she is dressed in a light cotton dress and has a kitchen apron on; JEAN comes in dressed in livery carrying a large pair of riding boots with spurs, which he puts down on the floor in view.

JEAN: Miss Julie's gone mad again this evening; completely mad!

KRISTIN: So, you're back now are you?

JEAN: I went with the Count to the station, and when I came back past the barn I went in and danced, and what do I see but the young mistress leading the dance with the gamekeeper? But when she noticed I was there, she rushes straight up to me and asks me to dance the ladies' waltz with her. And the way she danced – I've never seen the like. She's mad.

KRISTIN: She always has been, but never so much as these past two weeks, since the engagement broke up.

JEAN: Yes, what was it happened there? He was a decent young man, even though he wasn't rich. Ach! They've such airs. (*Sits at end of the table.*) It's queer though, a young mistress, ahem, who prefers to stay at home with the servants?, rather than go with her father to visit family?

KRISTIN: She's probably a bit embarrassed after that hullabaloo with her fiancé.

JEAN: Probably! He can hold his own anyway. Kristin, do you know how it happened? I saw it, you know, although I pretended not to.

KRISTIN: You didn't!

JEAN: Yes, I did. – They were in the stable yard one evening and the mistress was training him, as she put it – you know what happened? Well, she had him jumping over the whip like you teach a dog to jump. He jumped twice and she clipped him each time; but the third time he snatched the whip out of her hand, broke it into a thousand pieces and off he went.

KRISTIN: Is that what happened? You don't say!

JEAN: Yes, that was that! So what tasty morsel have you got for me, Kristin?

KRISTIN: (*Serving JEAN from saucepan.*) Just a bit of kidney that I cut off the joint!

JEAN: (*Smells the food.*) Smells lovely. *Mon grand délice.* (*Feels the plate.*) You could have warmed the plate though!

KRISTIN: You're fussier than the Count himself, once you get going. (*Tugs his hair affectionately.*)

JEAN: (*Angry.*) Don't pull my hair! You know how sensitive I am.

KRISTIN: There, there, it's only love, you know that. (*JEAN eats. KRISTIN gets out a bottle of beer.*)

JEAN: Beer on midsummer eve? No thank you very much! I've something better myself. (*Opens table drawer and takes out a bottle of red wine with a yellow seal.*) Yellow seal, see it? – Give me a glass now, a stem glass of course, when you're drinking it neat!

KRISTIN: (*Turns back to the stove and puts on a small saucepan.*) God preserve whoever gets you for a husband! Such a fusspot!

JEAN: You talk! You'd be happy enough, if you got a refined chap like me; and I don't think it does you any harm that they call me your fiancé! (*Takes the wine.*) Good! very good! Just a bit too chilled. (*Warms the glass within his hand.*) We bought this in Dijon. It was four francs a litre without the bottle; then there's the duty on top of that! – What are you boiling now? that's got such an infernal smell!

KRISTIN: Oh, just some damned thing Miss Julie wanted for Diana.

JEAN: You should express yourself more delicately, Kristin! Anyway why should you stand there working for that wretched dog on a holiday? Is it ill?

KRISTIN: Yes, it's ill! She's sneaked off with the gatekeeper's pug – and now she's in trouble – the mistress won't hear of it.

JEAN: The mistress is very haughty in such matters and has too little pride in others, exactly like the Countess when she was alive. She was most at home in the kitchen or in the barn, but she would never travel drawn by just one horse; she always had dirty cuffs, but wanted the crest on all the buttons. – Now the young mistress doesn't take care of herself, or her person. You could almost say she's not quite refined. Just now when she was dancing in the barn, she dragged the gamekeeper away from Anna and asked him to dance with her. We wouldn't do that, would we; but that's what happens when the gentry make themselves common – they become common! – But she is magnificent! Splendid! And what shoulders! and – etcetera!

KRISTIN: Oh yes, but I wouldn't overdo it! I've heard what Clara says who dresses her.

JEAN: Ah, Clara! You're all so jealous of each other! But I've been out riding with her...And then the way she dances!

KRISTIN: Listen, Jean! don't you want to dance with me, when I'm finished here?

JEAN: Yes, of course I do.

KRISTIN: Promise me?

JEAN: Promise? When I say I'll do a thing, I do it! Meanwhile, thank you for the meal. It was very nice! (*Puts the cork in the bottle.*)

MISS JULIE: (*In the doorway, calling off.*) I'll be back soon! Carry on, don't wait for me!

(*JEAN sneaks the bottle into the drawer, gets up respectfully.*)

MISS JULIE: (*Comes in; goes to KRISTIN at the stove.*) Well! is it ready?

(*KRISTIN indicates that JEAN is present.*)

JEAN: (*Gallantly.*) Do the ladies have secrets?

MISS JULIE: (*Hits JEAN in the face with her handkerchief.*) Nosy!

JEAN: Ah, what a lovely scent from that violet!

MISS JULIE: (*Coquettishly.*) Cheeky! So you know about perfumes too? You can certainly dance...there now, no peeping! go away!

JEAN: (*Nosy, polite.*) Is it a magic potion for midsummer eve, the ladies are making? Something to help you tell your fortune by the stars, and reveal future husbands!

MISS JULIE: (*Sharply.*) You'll need strong eyes, if you want to see that! (*To KRISTIN.*) Pour it into a bottle and cork it properly. – Come and dance a reel with me, Jean...

JEAN: (*Slowly.*) I don't want to be impolite to anyone, but I have promised Kristin this dance...

MISS JULIE: Well, she can have another; can't you, Kristin? Won't you lend Jean to me?

KRISTIN: It's not up to me. If the mistress condescends, it's not for him to refuse. Let him go! and be grateful for the honour.

JEAN: To be honest, not wanting to give offence, I wonder anyway if it's wise of the mistress to dance twice in a row with the same partner, particularly since these people aren't slow to jump to conclusions...

MISS JULIE: (*Flaring up.*) What? What kind of conclusions? What do you mean?

JEAN: (*Yielding.*) Since the mistress won't understand then I must speak more plainly. It looks bad to prefer one of the servants when the others await the same unusual honour...

MISS JULIE: Prefer! The very thought! I'm surprised! I, the mistress of the house, honour the servants' dance with my presence, and now when I really would like to dance, I would like to dance with someone who can lead, so I'm not made a laughing-stock.

JEAN: As madam commands! I am at your service!

MISS JULIE: (*Softly.*) Don't take it as an order! Tonight we are happy folk at a party, let's set all rank aside! So, offer me your arm now! – don't worry, Kristin! I won't take your fiancé away from you!

(*JEAN offers his arm and leads MISS JULIE out.*)

✱

Dumb Show

Played as though the actress was really alone in the theatre; turns her back to the audience when necessary; doesn't face out into the auditorium; doesn't rush for fear the audience will grow impatient.

KRISTIN is alone. There is faint fiddle music in the background, a Scottish rhythm. She hums to the music; clears the table after JEAN, washes the plate at the sink, dries it and puts it in a cupboard. Then she takes off her apron, takes out a small mirror from a table drawer, stands it against the lilac vase on the table; lights a tallow candle upon which she heats a curling iron, with which she curls the hair on her forehead. Then she goes to the door and listens. Returns to the table. Finds the mistress's forgotten handkerchief, which she picks up and smells; spreads it out, distracted, stretches it out, smooths it and folds it in four quarters and so on.

✱

JEAN: (*Comes in alone.*) She really is mad though! What a way to dance! while people stand smirking at her behind the door posts. What do you think, Kristin?

KRISTIN: It's her time of the month, and then she's always a bit strange. But do you want to come and dance with me now?

JEAN: You're not cross are you that I let you down...

KRISTIN: No! – Not for such a small thing, you know that; and I know my place too...

JEAN: (*Puts his arm round her waist.*) You're such a sensible girl, Kristin, and you'd make a good wife...

MISS JULIE: (*Comes in; unpleasantly surprised but with forced jocularity.*) You're a charming partner – running off from your lady.

JEAN: On the contrary, Miss Julie, as you see I have hurried back to fetch the one I abandoned!

MISS JULIE: (*Changes.*) You know, you dance like no one else! – But why are you in livery on a holiday! Take it off at once!

JEAN: Then I must ask your ladyship to absent herself a moment, because my black coat is hanging here... (*He makes a gesture to the right.*)

MISS JULIE: You're not shy in front of me, are you? Just to change a jacket! Go into your room then and come back! Or else stay, and I'll turn my back.

JEAN: With your permission then, Miss Julie! (*He goes off to the right; we see his arm as he changes jackets.*)

MISS JULIE: (*To KRISTIN.*) Kristin; is Jean your fiancé, since he's so familiar with you?

JEAN: Fiancé? If you like! We call it that.

MISS JULIE: Call it that?

KRISTIN: Well, the mistress has had a fiancé herself, and...

MISS JULIE: Yes, we were properly engaged...

KRISTIN: But nothing came of it anyway...
(*JEAN comes in wearing black frock-coat and black bowler hat.*)

MISS JULIE: *Très gentil; monsieur Jean! Très gentil.*

JEAN: *Vous voulez plaisanter, madame!*

MISS JULIE: *Et vous voulez parler français!* Where have you learnt that?

JEAN: In Switzerland, while I was wine waiter in one of the biggest hotels in Lucerne!

MISS JULIE: But you look like a gentleman in that frock-coat. *Charmant!* (*Sits at the table.*)

JEAN: Oh, you're just flattering me!

MISS JULIE: (*Shocked.*) Flattering you?

JEAN: My natural modesty forbids me to believe that you are being completely truthful to someone like me, and therefore I allowed myself to presume that you were exaggerating, or as you could put it, flattering!

MISS JULIE: Where did you learn to put words together like that? You must have been to the theatre a lot?

JEAN: Among other things! I've been to many places, I have!

MISS JULIE: But you were born here?

JEAN: My father was a farm hand at the public prosecutor's place just nearby, and I used to see you as a child, although you wouldn't have noticed me!

MISS JULIE: No, not at all!

JEAN: Yes, and I remember in particular one time...no, I couldn't tell about that!

MISS JULIE: Oh, please! Do tell. Go on. Just this once!

JEAN: No, I really couldn't now! Another time perhaps.

MISS JULIE: Another time is a cheat. Is it really so dangerous to tell it now?

JEAN: It's not dangerous, but I'd rather not! – Look at that! (*Indicates KRISTIN who has fallen asleep in a chair by the stove.*)

MISS JULIE: She'll make a nice wife, that one! Does she snore too?

JEAN: No, she doesn't, but she talks in her sleep.

MISS JULIE: (*Cynically.*) How do you know she talks in her sleep?

JEAN: (*Boldly.*) I've heard her!
(*Pause, during which they look at one another.*)

MISS JULIE: Why don't you sit down?

JEAN: I can't allow myself to do so in your presence!

MISS JULIE: But if I order you to?

JEAN: Then I obey!

MISS JULIE: Sit down then! – No, wait! Can you give me something to drink first?

JEAN: I don't know what we have in the icebox. I think there's only beer.

MISS JULIE: Don't say only! I have such simple tastes that I prefer it to wine.

JEAN: (*Gets out of the icebox a beer bottle, which he opens; gets a glass and plate from the cupboard and serves.*) At your service!

MISS JULIE: Thank you! Don't you want a drink yourself?

JEAN: I'm not a great lover of beer, but if the mistress orders me!

MISS JULIE: Order? – I think that as a polite partner you can keep your lady company.

JEAN: You are quite right! (*Opens a bottle, pours a glass.*)

MISS JULIE: Drink to me, now!

(*JEAN hesitates.*)

I think the poor lad is shy!

JEAN: (*On his knee, joking, parody; raising his glass.*) To your health, my mistress!

MISS JULIE: Bravo! – Now you must kiss my shoe and everything will be quite perfect.

(*JEAN hesitates but then boldly takes her foot, which he kisses lightly.*)

Excellent! You should have been an actor.

JEAN: (*Gets up.*) We must stop this! Miss Julie; someone might come in and see us.

MISS JULIE: What would that matter?

JEAN: People would talk, quite simply! And if you knew how their tongues were wagging up there, just now...

MISS JULIE: Whatever did they say! Tell me! – Sit down now!

JEAN: (*Sits.*) I don't want to offend you, but they used expressions – which cast suspicions, which...you can perhaps imagine yourself! You are no child, and when people see a lady drinking alone with a man – let alone a servant – at night – – then...

MISS JULIE: Then what! And besides we're not alone. Kristin is here.

JEAN: Yes, asleep!

MISS JULIE: Then I'll wake her. (*Gets up.*) Kristin! Are you asleep?

KRISTIN: (*In her sleep.*) Bla-bla-bla-bla.

MISS JULIE: Kristin! – She can certainly sleep!

KRISTIN: (*In her sleep.*) The Count's boots are brushed – put on the coffee – at once, at once, at once – oh oh – Phew!

MISS JULIE: (*Takes her by the nose.*) Will you wake up!

JEAN: (*Sternly.*) Don't disturb someone who's asleep!

MISS JULIE: (*Sharply.*) What?

JEAN: Someone who's been standing by the stove all day gets tired by nightfall. Sleep is to be respected...

MISS JULIE: (*Changes.*) That's very thoughtful, it does you credit – thank you! (*Gives him her hand.*) Come and pick some lilacs for me now!
(*During the following, KRISTIN wakes up and goes out sleepily right and goes to bed.*)
JEAN: With you, miss?
MISS JULIE: With me!
JEAN: That's not on! Absolutely not!
MISS JULIE: I can't imagine what you're thinking. Is it possible you are imagining something?
JEAN: No, not me, but people.
MISS JULIE: What? That I'm *verleibt* with the servant?
JEAN: I'm not a conceited man, but I have seen examples of it – and to these people nothing is sacred!
MISS JULIE: I do believe he's an aristocrat!
JEAN: Yes, I am.
MISS JULIE: Then, if I step down...
JEAN: Don't step down, Miss Julie, listen to my advice! There's no one who'd believe that you voluntarily descended; people will always say that you fell!
MISS JULIE: I have a higher opinion of people than you do! Come and see! – Come! (*She gazes at him.*) ᶜ
JEAN: Do you know you are strange!
MISS JULIE: Perhaps! But so are you! – Besides, everything is strange! Life, people, everything is a mess that drifts, drifts out into the water until it sinks, sinks! I have a dream that recurs now and again; which comes to mind now. I'm sitting on top of a pillar I've climbed and can see no possibility of getting down; I get giddy when I look down, and down I have to go, but I haven't the courage to throw myself down; I can't hold on up there and I'm longing to fall; but I don't fall. And I shall find no peace until I come down, no rest before I get down, down on the ground! And if I get down to the ground, I want to go under the ground...Have you ever known anything like that?
JEAN: No! I dream that I am lying under a tall tree in a dark wood. I want to climb up, up to the top and look about me across the bright landscape, where the sun

shines, to plunder the birds' nests up there, where the golden eggs are. And I climb and I climb, but the trunk is so thick and smooth, and it's such a long way to the first branch. But I know that if only I could reach the first branch, then I'd continue to the top as if I was on a ladder. I haven't reached it yet, but I will reach it, if it is only in my dream!

MISS JULIE: Here am I talking about dreams with you. Come on! Just into the gardens!

(*She offers him her arm and they go out.*)

JEAN: We shall sleep with nine wild midsummer flowers under our pillows, Miss Julie, and our dreams will come true!

(*They turn in the doorway. JEAN puts his hand over one eye.*)

MISS JULIE: Let me see what you've got in your eye!

JEAN: Oh, it's nothing – just a piece of dust – it will pass.

MISS JULIE: It was the sleeve of my dress brushed you; sit down now, and let me help you! (*Takes him by the arm and sits him down, takes his head and tips it back; with the corner of her handkerchief she tries to remove the piece of dust.*) Sit still now, quite still! (*She slaps his hand.*) Do what I say now! – I do believe he's shaking, the big strong man! (*She feels his upper arm.*) With such arms!

JEAN: (*Warning.*) Miss Julie!

MISS JULIE: Yes, Monsieur Jean.

JEAN: *Attention? Je ne suis qu'un homme!*

MISS JULIE: Will you sit still! – There! It's gone now! Kiss my hand and thank me!

JEAN: (*Stands up.*) Miss Julie! listen to me! – Kristin has gone to bed now! – Will you listen to me!

MISS JULIE: Kiss my hand first!

JEAN: Listen to me!

MISS JULIE: Kiss my hand first!

JEAN: Yes, but you'll have only yourself to blame!

MISS JULIE: For what?

JEAN: For what? Are you a child at twenty-five? Don't you know it's dangerous to play with fire?

MISS JULIE: Not for me; I'm insured!

JEAN: (*Boldly.*) No, you are not! And if you are, then there's inflammable equipment in the neighbourhood!

MISS JULIE: You mean you?

JEAN: Yes! Not because it's me, but because I am a young man –

MISS JULIE: With a handsome appearance – what incredible conceit! A Don Juan perhaps! Or a Josef! I think, upon my soul, you think you are a Josef!

JEAN: You think so?

MISS JULIE: I'm afraid so!
(*JEAN boldly goes and takes her round the waist to kiss her.*)
(*Slaps him round the face.*) Stop it!

JEAN: Is that serious or a joke?

MISS JULIE: Serious!

JEAN: Then that was also serious just now! You play far too seriously and that's what is dangerous! Now I'm tired of the game and if you'll excuse me I will return to my work. The Count wants his boots in good time and it's way past midnight.

MISS JULIE: Put away the boots!

JEAN: No! They are my job which I must do, but that doesn't include being your playmate, and never will do since I consider myself too good for that.

MISS JULIE: You're proud!

JEAN: In certain respects; not in others.

MISS JULIE: Have you ever been in love?

JEAN: We don't use that word, but I've been keen on many girls, and once I was ill from not being able to have the one I wanted: ill, you see, just like the princes in 'A Thousand and One Nights'! who couldn't eat or drink out of pure love!

MISS JULIE: Who was it?
(*JEAN keeps silent.*)
Who was it?

JEAN: You can't force me to say that.

MISS JULIE: If I ask you as an equal asks a – friend! Who was it?

JEAN: It was you!

111

MISS JULIE: (*Sits down.*) How priceless...

JEAN: Yes, if you like! It was ridiculous! You see, it was that story I didn't want to tell you just now, but now I will!

Do you know what the world looks like from down there – no, you don't! Like hawks and falcons, those one hardly ever sees the backs of because they are mostly soaring about up there somewhere! I lived in the labourer's cottage with seven brothers and sisters, and a pig out in the stony meadow where not a tree would grow! But from the windows I saw the walls of the Count's estate and the apple trees rising above it. It was the Garden of Eden; and many evil angels stood there with flaming swords guarding it. But none the less for that had I and other boys found the path to the tree of life – now you despise me?

MISS JULIE: Ah! All boys steal apples.

JEAN: You can say that now, but you despise me anyway! So be it! Once I came into the gardens with my mother to weed the onion patch. Beside the vegetable plot stood a Turkish pavilion in the shade of jasmine overgrown with honeysuckle. I didn't know what it was for, but I'd never seen such a beautiful building. People went in and came out again, and one day the door was left open. I crept in and saw the walls covered with pictures of kings and emperors, and there were red curtains at the windows with tassels on – now you know what I mean. I – – – (*Breaks off a lilac flower and holds it under MISS JULIE's nose.*) – I had never been inside the house, never seen anything except the church – but this was more beautiful; and wherever my thoughts strayed, they always returned – there. And gradually there arose in me a longing to one day experience the full delight of – *enfin*, I sneaked in, saw and marvelled. But someone was coming! There was only one way out for gentlefolk, but for me there was another, and I had no choice but to take it! (*MISS JULIE, who has taken the lilac, lets it fall on to the table.*) Then I started to run, crashed through some raspberry canes, charged across a strawberry patch and came out on to a terrace with a rose garden. There I saw a pink dress and a pair of white stockings – it was you. I lay down under a pile of weeds, I wonder if you can imagine, beneath thistles that pricked me and damp earth that stank. And I watched you as you walked among the roses, and I thought: if it is true that a thief can enter heaven and be with the angels, then it's strange that a farm labourer's child here on God's earth can't come into the grounds of the manor and play with the Count's daughter!

MISS JULIE: (*Elegiac.*) Do you think all poor children have the same thoughts as you did then?

JEAN: (*First hesitating, then with conviction.*) Do all poor – yes – of course they do! Of course!

MISS JULIE: Then it must be an immense sorrow to be poor!

JEAN: (*With deep pain, strongly charged.*) Oh, Miss Julie! oh! – A dog can lie on the Countess's sofa, a horse can have its nose stroked by the mistress's hand, but a labourer – (*Changes.*) – ah well, one or two have the mettle to hoist themselves up in the world, but how often is that! – Meanwhile, do you know what I did! – I ran into the mill stream with my clothes on; was dragged out and beaten. But the following Sunday, when my father and everyone else went off to my grandma's, I fixed it so that I would stay home. So I washed myself with soap and hot water, put on my best clothes and walked to church, where I would be able to see you! I saw you and went home, resolved to die; but I wanted a beautiful and pleasant death, without pain. And then I remembered it was dangerous to sleep under an elder bush. We had a big one, that was just in bloom. I stripped it of everything it had, and bedded down in the oat bin. Have you noticed how smooth oats are? soft to the touch like human skin...? Anyway I closed the lid and shut my eyes; fell asleep and awoke really very ill. But I didn't die, as you can see.

What I intended – I don't know! There was no hope of winning you anyway – but you were a sign, of how hopeless it was that I should ever rise above the station I was born into.

MISS JULIE: You tell the story charmingly, you know! Have you been to school?

JEAN: A little; but I have read many novels and gone to the theatre. Besides I have heard the gentry speak, and it's from them I have learned most.

MISS JULIE: Do you stand listening to what we are saying!

JEAN: Of course! And I've heard a lot, too! sitting on the coachman's box, rowing the boat. Once I heard you Miss Julie and a friend...

MISS JULIE: Oh! – What did you hear?

JEAN: Ah well, that wouldn't be nice to say; but I suppose I was a little surprised, and couldn't understand where you learnt all the words. Perhaps after all there is not such a big difference, as one thinks, between people and people!

MISS JULIE: For shame! We don't behave like you do, when we are engaged!

JEAN: (*Stares at her.*) Are you sure? Yes, you don't have to pretend innocence to me...

MISS JULIE: He was a wretch, I gave my love to.

JEAN: You always say that – afterwards.

MISS JULIE: Always?

JEAN: I think so, always, since I've heard that expression several times before on similar occasions.

MISS JULIE: What occasions?

JEAN: Like the one in question! Last time I...

MISS JULIE: (*Stands up.*) Quiet! I don't want to hear any more!

JEAN: Neither did she – it's remarkable. Well then, I must ask to be excused so I can go to bed.

MISS JULIE: (*Softly.*) Go to bed on midsummer eve!

JEAN: Yes! Dancing with that rabble up there really doesn't interest me.

MISS JULIE: Get the key to the boathouse and row me out on to the lake; I want to see the sunrise!

JEAN: Is that wise?

MISS JULIE: It sounds as though you are afraid for your reputation!

JEAN: Why not? I've no desire to be made a fool of, no desire to be dismissed without references, when I decide to establish myself. And I think I have a certain duty towards Kristin.

MISS JULIE: I see. So it's Kristin now...

JEAN: Yes, but it's also you. – Follow my advice and go to bed!

MISS JULIE: Am I to do as you say?

JEAN: For once; for your own sake! I beg you! It's getting late, sleepiness makes you drunk, and hot-headed! Go to bed! Besides – if I'm not mistaken – they're coming looking for me! And if they find us here you're lost!

CHOIR: (*Approaches singing.*)
From the woods two wives came walking
Fa-la-ra.
The one of them's legs were soaking
Fa-la-ray.

They talked of a hundred bright shillings
Fa-la-ra.
But between them they hadn't a farthing
Fa-la-ray.

I'll leave you this wreath at parting
Fa-la-ra.
For another girl's my darling
Fa-la-ray!

MISS JULIE: I know these people, and I love them, just as they are fond of me. Let them come in, you'll see!

JEAN: No, Miss Julie, they don't love you. They take your food, but they spit after it! Believe me! Listen to them, just listen to what they're singing! – No, don't listen to them!

MISS JULIE: (*Listening.*) What are they singing?

JEAN: It's a dirty song! About you and me!

MISS JULIE: How vile! Urgh! And so treacherous! –

JEAN: The rabble are always cowardly! And in battle with them it is best to run away!

MISS JULIE: Run away? But where? We can't get out! And we can't go in to Kristin!

JEAN: So! Into my room then? Necessity has no conventions; and you can trust me, because I am your true, loyal and respectful friend.

MISS JULIE: But suppose! – suppose they look for you there?

JEAN: I'll bolt the door, and if they try to break in, I'll shoot them! – Come on! (*On his knees.*) Come!

MISS JULIE: (*Intently.*) You promise me...?

JEAN: I swear!

> (*MISS JULIE goes out hastily to the right. JEAN hurries after her.*)

*

Ballet

The FARM PEOPLE in their Sunday best, with flowers in their hats; A FIDDLER at their head; a cask of small beer and a small keg of brandy, decorated with leaves, set upon the table; glasses are taken out. They drink. Then they form a ring and sing and dance dancing games to the above song.

When this is over, they leave again, singing.

*

MISS JULIE comes in alone; sees the mess in the kitchen; clasps her hands together; then she takes out a powder puff and powders her face.

JEAN: (*Comes in, agitated.*) There, you've seen! And you've heard! Do you think it's possible to stay here?

MISS JULIE: No! I don't think it is. But what shall we do then!

JEAN: Go away, travel far away from here!

MISS JULIE: Travel? Yes, but where?

JEAN: To Switzerland, to the Italian lakes; you've never been there, have you?

MISS JULIE: No! Is it beautiful there?

JEAN: Oh, one endless summer, oranges, laurel trees, oh!

MISS JULIE: But what would we do there?

JEAN: I would set up a hotel there, top-class quality for top-class customers.

MISS JULIE: A hotel?

JEAN: It's a good life, believe me; endless new faces, new languages; not a minute's spare time for worry or nerves; no wondering what to do next – there the work finds itself; the bell ringing night and day, the train whistling, the omnibus coming and going; while the golden coins roll into the till. What a life!

MISS JULIE: Yes, that's the way to live! And me?

JEAN: The mistress of the house; the jewel of the establishment. With your looks...and your style – oh – it's a guaranteed success! Marvellous! You'll sit like a queen in the office putting the slaves to work with the flick of an electric switch; the guests will file past your throne and humbly set their tribute on the table – you wouldn't believe how people tremble when they are handed the bill – I'll salt the bills and you sugar them with your sweetest smile – ach! let's get away from here – (*Takes out a timetable from his pocket.*) – At once, on the next train! – we'll be in Malmö at six thirty; Hamburg at eight forty in the morning: Frankfurt to Basle takes one day, and we'll be in Como by the Gothard Pass in, let me see, three days. Three days!

MISS JULIE: All that is fine. But, Jean – you must give me courage – Say that you love me! Come and embrace me!

JEAN: (*Hesitantly.*) I want to – but I daren't! Not in this house any more. I love you – without a doubt – do you doubt it, Miss Julie?

MISS JULIE: (*Truly feminine.*) 'Miss Julie'! – Say 'Julie'! There mustn't be any barriers between us any more! – Call me Julie.[1]

JEAN: (*Tortured.*) I can't! – There are still barriers between us, so long as we stay in this house – there is the past, there is the Count – and I've never met anyone I've had so much respect for – I only need to see his gloves on a chair, to feel small – I only need to hear the bell ring from up there, and I jump like a startled horse – and when I see his boots standing there so upright and true, my flesh creeps! (*Kicks the boots.*) Superstition and

---

[1] These two speeches concern the polite and familiar form of address in the original.

prejudice, which they taught us from childhood – but which could be forgotten just as easily. Just come to another country, to a republic, and they crawl before my porter's livery – you're supposed to crawl, all right! but I won't! I'm not born to fall on my face, I'm of better mettle; I've got character, just let me get to the first branch, then you'll see me climb! I'm a servant today, but next year I'll be a proprietor, in ten years I'll be a gentleman, and then I'll go to Romania and have myself decorated, and I could – mark me carefully I say can – end up a count!

MISS JULIE: Lovely, lovely!

JEAN: Oh, in Romania you can buy a title, and you'd be a countess too! My countess!

MISS JULIE: What do I care for all that, that I'm leaving behind me now! – Say that you love me, otherwise – yes, what am I otherwise?

JEAN: I'll tell you, a thousand times – later! Just not here! And above all, no emotions, or all will be lost! We must act coolly, like sensible people. (*Picks up a cigar, snips it, lights it.*) Now, sit down there! and I'll sit down here, and we'll talk, as if nothing had happened.

MISS JULIE: (*Despairing.*) Oh, my God! Haven't you any feelings!

JEAN: Me! There is no one more feeling than I; but I can control myself.

MISS JULIE: You could kiss my shoe a moment ago – and now!

JEAN: (*Hard.*) Yes, that was then! Now we've other things to think about.

MISS JULIE: Don't speak harshly to me!

JEAN: No, but sensibly! We've been reckless once, let's not be reckless again! The Count could be here any minute and we must decide our destinies before then. What do you think of my plans for the future? Do you like them?

MISS JULIE: They seem reasonable – but just one question; such a large enterprise requires a large amount of capital; have you got it?

JEAN: (*Bites his cigar.*) Me! Of course! I have my trades, my vast experience, my knowledge of languages! That's good enough as capital, I trust!

MISS JULIE: But you can't buy even a train ticket with it.

JEAN: That is, of course, true; but that's why I'm looking for a partner, who can advance the funds!

MISS JULIE: Where will you find one so quickly?

JEAN: That's what you can do if you are to be my companion!

MISS JULIE: I can't, and I don't own anything myself.
(*Pause.*)

JEAN: Then the whole thing collapses...

MISS JULIE: And...

JEAN: Things stay as they are!

MISS JULIE: Do you think I can stay under this roof as your mistress? Do you think I'll let people point the finger at me; do you think I can look my father in the eye after this? No! Take me away from here, from the humiliation and dishonour! – Oh, what have I done, my God, my God! (*Cries.*)

JEAN: There there, so you're singing that song now! – what have you done? The same as many others before you!

MISS JULIE: (*Screaming in a fit.*) And now you despise me! – I'm falling, I'm falling!

JEAN: Fall down to me, and I'll lift you up again!

MISS JULIE: What terrible force drew me to you? The weak to the strong? The falling to the ascending! Or was it love? Love – that? Do you know what love is?

JEAN: Me? Yes, I can assure you; don't you think I've done it before?

MISS JULIE: What language you use, and what thoughts you think!

JEAN: It's what I've learnt, and it's what I am! Don't be nervous now and don't put on airs, for we're birds of a feather now! – There there, poor little girl, come on, I'll give you a glass of something special! (*Opens the table drawer and takes out the wine bottle; fills two used glasses.*)

MISS JULIE: Where did you get that from?

JEAN: The cellar!

MISS JULIE: My father's burgundy!

JEAN: Isn't it suitable for the son-in-law?

MISS JULIE: And I'm drinking beer! Me!

JEAN: That shows simply that you have got worse taste than me.

MISS JULIE: Thief!

JEAN: Are you going to tell?

MISS JULIE: Oh, oh! Accomplice to a house thief! Have I been drunk, have I been walking in my sleep tonight! midsummer eve! Festival of innocent games...

JEAN: Innocent, hm!

MISS JULIE: (*Pacing up and down.*) Is there anyone on earth this moment, more unhappy than I am!

JEAN: Why are you? After such a conquest! Think of Kristin in there! Don't you think she's got feelings too!

MISS JULIE: I thought so earlier, but I don't think so any more! Labourers are labourers...

JEAN: And whores are whores!

MISS JULIE: (*On her knees with hands clasped.*) O, God in heaven, end my wretched life! Take me away from this filth I'm sinking into! Save me! Save me!

JEAN: I can't deny that I feel sorry for you! When I lay in the onion patch and saw you in the rose garden, then... I'll tell you now...I had the same dirty thoughts that all boys have.

MISS JULIE: You, who wanted to die for me?

JEAN: In the oat bin? That was just talk.

MISS JULIE: Lies then!

JEAN: (*Beginning to grow sleepy.*) More or less! I read the story in a newspaper about a chimney sweep, who laid himself down in a firewood bin with lilacs, because he'd been taken to court for maintenance...

MISS JULIE: I see, you're one of those...

JEAN: What else could I come up with; You're always meant to woo women with fine words!

MISS JULIE: Wretch!

JEAN: *Merde!*

MISS JULIE: And now you've seen the hawk's back...

JEAN: Not the back exactly...

MISS JULIE: And I'm intended to be the first branch...

JEAN: But the branch was rotten...

MISS JULIE: I was to be the hotel sign...

JEAN: And me the hotel...

MISS JULIE: Sit behind your counter, attract your customers, falsify your bills...

JEAN: I'd do that myself...

MISS JULIE: That a human heart can be so thoroughly dirty!

JEAN: Clean it then!

MISS JULIE: Lackey, Domestic, stand up when I'm speaking!

JEAN: Domestic's mistress, lackey's slut, shut your mouth and get out of here. You come here and complain that I'm coarse? None of my kind would behave as coarsely as you have this evening. Do you think any maid would accost men like you have? Have you ever seen any girl from my class offer herself around in that way? I've only seen it among animals and fallen women!

MISS JULIE: (*Crushed.*) You're right; hit me; trample me; I haven't deserved any better. I'm a wretch; but help me! Help me out of this if there's any way at all!

JEAN: (*More mildly.*) I won't disgrace myself by denying my part in the honour of seducing you; but do you think anyone in my position would have dared so much as to lift his eyes to you, if you didn't invite it! I'm still surprised...

MISS JULIE: And proud...

JEAN: Why not? While I must confess that the conquest was too easy to have been much of a thrill.

MISS JULIE: Beat me more!

JEAN: (*Stands.*) No! Forgive me instead for what I have said! I don't hit defenceless people, least of all a woman. I can't deny that on the one hand it pleases me to see that it was just gilding that dazzled us down here, to have seen the hawk's back was just grey too, that there was powder on those soft fine cheeks, and that there could be dirt beneath those polished nails, that the handkerchief was dirty, though it smelled of perfume...! but it pains me on the other hand to see that what I myself strived for, wasn't something more exalted, substantial; it pains me to see you sunk so low, that you are far beneath your cook; it pains me as it pains me to see the autumn flowers beaten by the rain and turned to dirt.

MISS JULIE: You speak as if you were already above me?

JEAN: I am: you see I could make you a countess, but you could never make me a count.

MISS JULIE: But I am born of a count, and that you can never be!

JEAN: That's true; but I could father noblemen – if...

MISS JULIE: But you are a thief; I'm not.

JEAN: A thief is not the worst! There are worse things to be! And besides: when I serve in a house, I consider myself in a certain way a member of the family, like a child of the house, and you don't call it theft when a child pinches berries from a burgeoning bush! (*His passion re-awakens.*) Miss Julie, you are a lovely woman, altogether too good for someone like me! You've been the victim of intoxication, and you want to hide the mistake by imagining you are in love with me! You're not, unless possibly my exterior attracts you – and then your love is no better than mine – but I can never be satisfied with just being the animal for you, and I can never awaken love in you.

MISS JULIE: Are you sure of that?

JEAN: You mean that it's possible! – That I can love you, there's no doubt! You are beautiful, you are refined – (*Goes to her and takes her hand.*) – educated, lovable when you want to be, and once you've lighted a man's flame it will likely never be extinguished. (*Puts his arms around her waist.*) You are like mulled wine with its strong spices, one kiss from you... (*He tries to steer her out but she slowly pulls free.*)

MISS JULIE: Leave me alone! – You don't win me like that!

JEAN: How then? – Not in that way! Not caresses and fine words; not concern for the future, salvation from humiliation! How then?

MISS JULIE: How? How? I don't know? – not at all!
I loathe you the way I loathe rats, but I can't escape
from you!

JEAN: Escape with me!

MISS JULIE: (*Straightens herself.*) Escape? Yes, we shall
escape! – but I'm so tired! Give me a glass of wine!
(*JEAN pours out some wine.*)
(*Looks at her watch.*) But we'll talk first; we still have a bit
of time. (*Drinks from the glass, holds it out for more.*)

JEAN: Don't drink so much, you'll get drunk!

MISS JULIE: What would that matter?

JEAN: What would it matter? It's vulgar to get drunk! –
What were you going to say to me?

MISS JULIE: We shall escape! But we'll talk first, that is,
I'll talk because only you have been talking so far. You
told me your life, now I'll tell you mine, then we'll truly
know each other, before we begin our travels together.

JEAN: One moment! Forgive me! Think carefully, you
might regret it afterwards, you tell me your secrets at
a price.

MISS JULIE: Aren't you my friend?

JEAN: Yes, sometimes! But don't rely on me.

MISS JULIE: You're just saying that; – and besides: my
secrets are known to all. – You see, my mother was of
common extraction, very simple people. She was
brought up in the wisdom of the day about equality,
liberation for women and all that; and she had a distinct
aversion to marriage. When, therefore, my father
proposed to her, she replied that she would never be his
wife, but…he could be her lover. He told her he did not
want to see the woman he loved enjoy less respect than
himself. But she declared that the world's respect did not
interest her and under the influence of his passion, he
accepted her conditions. But then he was cut off from his
social circle and restricted to his domestic life, which
however couldn't satisfy him. I came into the world,
against my mother's will, as far as I can see; then I was
to be brought up by my mother, as a child of nature!

And into the bargain learnt all that a boy would learn, so that I'd be an example of how women are as good as men – I had to wear boys' clothes, and learn to look after horses, though I wasn't allowed in the cowshed. I had to groom and saddle, learn farming and go hunting, even to slaughter animals – that was horrible. And on the estate – men were set to do women's work, and women to do men's – with the consequence that the estate was going under, and we were the laughing-stock of the district. In the end my father must have woken up from the spell and rebelled so that everything was changed as he wanted. Then my parents were quietly married. My mother became ill – what illness it was I don't know – but she often had fits, hid herself in the attic and in the garden and could sometimes be out all night. Then there was the big fire which you've heard talked about. The house, the stables and the cowshed burnt up and under such strange circumstances that arson was suspected, for the accident happened the day after the quarter-yearly insurance expired, and the next premium sent by my father was delayed, due to the messenger's carelessness, and it didn't get there on time. (*She fills her glass and drinks.*)

JEAN: Don't drink any more!

MISS JULIE: Oh, what does it matter! – We were left penniless and had to sleep in the carriages. My father didn't know where he'd get the money to rebuild the house because he had had to give up his old friends who then forgot him. Then mother gave him the idea of asking for a loan from a childhood friend of hers, a brick manufacturer nearby. Father borrowed the money, but didn't have to pay interest, which surprised him. And so the house was rebuilt! – (*Drinks again.*) Do you know who burnt the house down?

JEAN: Your good mother!

MISS JULIE: Do you know who the brick manufacturer was?

JEAN: Your mother's lover?

MISS JULIE: Do you know whose the money was?

JEAN: Wait a second – no, that I don't know?

MISS JULIE: It was my mother's!

JEAN: The Count's that is to say, if there wasn't a marriage settlement?

MISS JULIE: There was no settlement! – My mother had a little capital, she didn't want to be under my father's control, and so she lodged it with her – friend.

JEAN: Who pinched it!

MISS JULIE: Quite right! He kept it! – This all came to my father's knowledge; he couldn't go to court, couldn't pay his wife's lover, couldn't prove it was his wife's money! – It was my mother's revenge for him taking control of the household. – At that time he was on the verge of shooting himself! – there was a rumour that he tried and failed! But he recovered, and my mother had to pay the price for her actions! They were five terrible years for me, I can tell you! I loved my father, but I took my mother's side, since I didn't know the circumstances. From her I had learnt mistrust and hatred of men – because she hated men as you've heard – and I swore to her never to become a slave to a man.

JEAN: And so you got engaged to the county bailiff!

MISS JULIE: Exactly, because he was to become my slave.

JEAN: And he didn't want to?

MISS JULIE: He did want to, but I didn't let him! I was tired of him.

JEAN: I saw that – in the stable yard?

MISS JULIE: What did you see?

JEAN: What did I see – how he broke off the engagement.

MISS JULIE: That's a lie! It was I who broke it off! Has he said it was him, the wretch?

JEAN: I'm sure he was no wretch! You hate men, Miss Julie?

MISS JULIE: Yes! – Most of them! But sometimes – in times of weakness, oh fie!

JEAN: You hate me too?

MISS JULIE: Immensely! I would like to have you killed like a beast...

JEAN: 'The offender gets two years penal servitude and the animal is shot'. Is that it?

MISS JULIE: That's right!

JEAN: But just now there's no prosecutor – and no dog! What shall we do then?

MISS JULIE: Go away!

JEAN: To torture each other to death?

MISS JULIE: No – to enjoy ourselves, two days, eight days, as long as we can enjoy ourselves, and then – die...

JEAN: Die? How stupid! In which case I'd rather set up a hotel.

MISS JULIE: (*Not hearing JEAN.*) – by Lake Como, where the sun always shines, where the laurel trees go into bud at Christmas and the oranges glisten.

JEAN: Lake Como is a rainy hole, and I didn't see any oranges there other than in the grocers' shops; but it's a good tourist spot, because there are a lot of villas to hire out to loving couples, and it's a very profitable business – do you know why – ? Well, they make the rental contract for six months – and then they leave after three weeks!

MISS JULIE: (*Naively.*) Why after three weeks?

JEAN: They quarrel of course! but the rent has to be paid in full all the same! And then you rent the place out again. And so it goes time after time, for love is powerful – even though it doesn't last very long!

MISS JULIE: You don't want to die with me?

JEAN: I don't want to die at all! Both because I enjoy living and because I consider suicide to be a crime against providence that has given us life.

MISS JULIE: You believe in God, *you?*

JEAN: Of course I do! And I go to church every other Sunday. – Now, to be honest, I'm tired of all this and I'm going to bed.

MISS JULIE: I see, and you think I'll settle for that? Do you know what a man owes a woman whom he has shamed?

JEAN: (*Takes out his purse and throws a silver coin on the table.*) Here you are! I wouldn't like to be owing you anything!

MISS JULIE: (*Pretending not to have noticed the insult.*) Do you know what the law states...

JEAN: Unfortunately the law doesn't specify any punishment for women who seduce men!

MISS JULIE: Do you see any other way out other than that we go away together, get married and separate?

JEAN: And if I refuse to join in this misalliance?

MISS JULIE: Misalliance...

JEAN: Yes, for me! You see: I have a better lineage than you, because I don't have any arsonists in my family!

MISS JULIE: How do you know?

JEAN: You can't know to the contrary, because we have no family records – except with the police! But I've read about your family tree in a book on the drawing-room table. Do you know who your ancestor was? He was a miller, who let the king sleep with his wife during the Danish war. I've no ancestors like that! I haven't any at all, but I can become one myself!

MISS JULIE: This is what I get in return for opening my heart to one who is unworthy, for giving away my family's honour...

JEAN: Dishonour! – Yes, you see, I said it! You shouldn't drink, it makes you talk! And one shouldn't talk!

MISS JULIE: Oh, how I regret it! – How I regret it! – If at least you loved me!

JEAN: For the last time – what do you mean? Should I cry, should I jump over a whip, should I kiss you, lure you away to Lake Como for three weeks and then...what shall I do? what do you want? this is beginning to become embarrassing! But that's what happens when you stick your nose into women's affairs! Miss Julie, I see that you are unhappy, I know that you are suffering, but I can't understand you. We don't have your affectations; there is no hate between us! We love as a game, when work allows us time; but we don't have all day and all night as you do! I consider you to be ill; decidedly ill.

MISS JULIE: You must be kind to me, and talk to me like a human being.

JEAN: Yes, but be a human being yourself! You spit at me and then won't allow me to dry myself – on you!

MISS JULIE: Help me, help me; just tell me what I should do – where I should go?

JEAN: In Jesus' name, if I only knew myself!

MISS JULIE: I've been out of my mind, I've been mad, but does that mean there can't be any salvation!

JEAN: Stay and be calm! No one knows anything.

MISS JULIE: Impossible! The servants know and Kristin knows!

JEAN: They don't know, and they'd never believe the like!

MISS JULIE: (*Slowly.*) But – it could happen again!

JEAN: That's true!

MISS JULIE: And the consequences?

JEAN: (*Scared.*) The consequences! – What have I been about, not thinking of that? Yes then, there's only one – away from here! At once! I won't go with you because then all is lost, no, you must go alone – away – anywhere!

MISS JULIE: Alone? Where? – I can't!

JEAN: You must! And before the Count comes back! If you stay, we know what will happen! A mistake once made, is willingly made again, since the damage is already done...You become bolder and bolder and – until in the end you stand exposed! So go! Write to the Count later and confess everything, except that it was me! And he can't very well guess that! And I shouldn't think either that he'd be anxious to know!

MISS JULIE: I'll go, if you come too!

JEAN: Are you mad, woman? Miss Julie runs off with her servant! It would be in the papers the day after tomorrow, and the Count would never survive that!

MISS JULIE: I can't go! I can't stay! Help me! I'm so tired, so terribly tired. – Order me! Set me in motion, I can't think any more, I can't act...!

JEAN: You see what a useless creature you are! Why do you preen yourselves and stick your noses in the air as if you were the lords of creation! Well: I'll order you! Go up and get dressed; provide yourself with travel money and then come down!

MISS JULIE: (*In a half whisper.*) Come up with me!

JEAN: Into your room? – You're mad! (*Hesitates a moment.*) No! Go at once! (*Takes her hand and leads her out.*)

MISS JULIE: (*As she leaves.*) Speak kindly to me, Jean!

JEAN: Orders always sound unfriendly; Now you know how it feels! Now you know!

(*Alone; heaves a sigh of relief; sits at the table; takes out a notebook and a pen; counts aloud now and then, mime-play of expressions, until KRISTIN comes in dressed for church, with a shirt front and a white cravat in her hand.*)

KRISTIN: Lord Jesus, what a mess! What have you been up to?

JEAN: Ah, it was Miss Julie dragged them all in here. Were you so fast asleep, you didn't hear anything?

KRISTIN: I slept like a log!

JEAN: Dressed for church already?

KRISTIN: Yes! You promised to go to Communion with me today!

JEAN: Oh yes, so I did! – And you've got the costume! Come on then!

(*Sits. KRISTIN dresses him shirt front and white cravat.*)

(*Sleepily.*) What's the lesson today?

KRISTIN: Well I imagine it's about John the Baptist getting his throat cut.

JEAN: That's going to be terribly long! – Oh, you're strangling me! – Oh, I'm so sleepy, so sleepy!

KRISTIN: Yes, well, what have you been doing up all night; you're quite green in the face?

JEAN: I've been sitting here talking with Miss Julie.

KRISTIN: She doesn't know how to behave, that girl!

(*Pause.*)

JEAN: (*Slowly.*) Kristin!

KRISTIN: Well?

JEAN: It's strange, isn't it, when you think of it. – Her!

KRISTIN: What's so strange?

JEAN: Everything!

(*Pause.*)

KRISTIN: (*Looks at the half-empty glasses on the table.*) Have you been drinking together too?

JEAN: Yes!

KRISTIN: For shame! – Look into my eyes!

JEAN: Yes!

KRISTIN: Is it possible? Is it possible?

JEAN: (*Thinks about it.*) Yes! It is!

KRISTIN: Urgh! I would never have believed it! No, for shame! For shame!

JEAN: You're not jealous of her are you?

KRISTIN: Not of her, no! If it had been Clara or Sofi; then I would have scratched your eyes out! – Yes, that's the way it is; why I don't know. – No, it's disgusting.

JEAN: Are you angry with her, then!

KRISTIN: No, with you! That was bad of you, very bad! Poor girl! – No, do you know what! I don't want to stay in this house; when we can no longer respect our masters.

JEAN: Why should we respect them?

KRISTIN: Yes, you tell me, you're so smart! But you don't want to serve people who behave indecently do you? You bring disgrace on yourself, that's what I think.

JEAN: Yes, but it's a comfort for us, isn't it, to realise they are no better than us!

KRISTIN: No, I don't agree; because if they're no better, then there's no point striving to better ourselves. – And think of the Count! Who has had so much sorrow in his life, Lord Jesus! No, I don't want to stay in this house any longer! – And with someone like you! If it had been that young bailiff; if it had been a better man...

JEAN: What?

KRISTIN: Oh yes! You're all right in yourself, but there is a difference between folk and folk after all. – No, I can never forget this. – The young mistress who was so proud, so haughty towards the menfolk, you'd never think she'd go out and give herself – – – and to such a man! Her! Who was going to have poor Diana shot for going with the gatekeeper's pug! – Yes, I don't mind saying it! – But I don't want to stay here, and on the twenty-fourth of October I'm off.

JEAN: And then?

KRISTIN: Well, since it's come up, isn't it about time you looked for something, since we're going to get married.

JEAN: Well, what should I look for? I couldn't get a position like this if I were married.

KRISTIN: No, of course not! Then you can become a porter or apply to be a caretaker at a government office. Civil service jobs don't pay well, but they are secure, and the wife and children get a pension...

JEAN: (*Grimacing.*) That's all very nice, but I don't intend to go dying for my wife and children just yet. I must confess that I really had somewhat grander plans.

KRISTIN: Your grand plans, yes! you've got responsibilities too! Think of them!

JEAN: Don't irritate me by talking about responsibilities, I know well enough what I have to do! (*Listens off.*) We've got plenty of time to think about this anyway. Go in now and get ready, so we can go to church.

KRISTIN: Who's wandering about up there?

JEAN: I don't know do I, unless it's Clara.

KRISTIN: (*Goes.*) It can't be the Count can it, come home without anyone hearing him?

JEAN: (*Afraid.*) The Count? No, I can't believe that, he would have rung.

KRISTIN: (*Goes.*) Well, God help us! I've never known the like.

(*The sun has come up and shines on the tree tops in the estate; the light moves gradually, until it shines obliquely through the windows.*

JEAN goes to the door and makes a sign.)

MISS JULIE: (*In travelling clothes with a small birdcage covered with a hand towel, which she puts on a chair.*) I'm ready.

JEAN: Ssh! Kristin is awake!

MISS JULIE: (*Extremely nervous throughout the following.*) Does she suspect anything?

JEAN: She doesn't know a thing! But my God, what do you look like!

MISS JULIE: What do I look like?

JEAN: You're as pale as a corpse and – sorry, but your face is dirty.

MISS JULIE: Let me wash then! – There! (*She goes to the washbasin and washes her face and hands.*) Give me a towel! – Oh – the sun's coming up!

JEAN: And the troll bursts![1]

MISS JULIE: Yes, the trolls have been out tonight! – But, Jean, listen! Come with me, I've got money now!

JEAN: (*Doubtful.*) Enough?

MISS JULIE: Enough to start with! Come with me, I can't travel alone, today. Imagine, midsummer day, in a stuffy train, packed in with loads of people staring at me; standing still at the stations when you long just to get away. No, I can't, I can't! And then the memories; childhood memories of midsummer days in the church, hung about with leaves – birch leaves and lilacs; dinner at the big table, relations, friends; afternoons in the grounds, dancing, music, flowers and games! Oh! you can run away, run, but the memories follow in the luggage van, and regrets and pangs of conscience.

JEAN: I'll come with you – but now, at once, before it's too late. Now this moment!

MISS JULIE: Get dressed then! (*Picks up birdcage.*)

JEAN: But no luggage! It would give us away!

MISS JULIE: No, nothing! Just what fits into the compartment.

JEAN: (*Picks up his hat.*) What have you got there? What is it?

MISS JULIE: It's just my greenfinch! I don't want to leave that!

JEAN: Oh, I see! We're going to have a birdcage with us now! You're insane aren't you! Put the cage down!

MISS JULIE: The only thing I'm bringing from home; the only living creature that likes me, since Diana was unfaithful to me! Don't be cruel! Let me take it with me!

JEAN: Put the cage down, I say – and don't speak so loudly. – Kristin will hear us!

MISS JULIE: No, I won't leave it in strange hands! I'd rather you kill it!

JEAN: Give the blighter to me then, and I'll wring its neck!

MISS JULIE: Yes, but don't hurt it! No...no, I can't.

JEAN: Give it here; I can!

MISS JULIE: (*Takes the bird out of the cage and kisses it.*) Oh, my little Serine, are you going to die and leave your mistress now?

[1] In popular myth a troll explodes or bursts if exposed to sunlight.

JEAN: Please don't make any scenes; your life is at stake, your welfare! Here, quickly!
(*Snatches the bird from her; takes it to the chopping block and picks up the kitchen cleaver. MISS JULIE turns away.*)
You should have learnt to kill chickens instead of shooting with a revolver – (*Chops.*) – then you wouldn't faint at just a drop of blood!

MISS JULIE: (*Screams.*) Kill me too! Kill me. You who can kill an innocent animal without your hand even shaking. Oh, how I hate and despise you; there's blood between us! I curse the moment I saw you, I curse the moment I was conceived in my mother's womb!

JEAN: What's the point in your cursing! Go!

MISS JULIE: (*Approaching the chopping block, as if drawn there against her will.*) No, I don't want to go yet; I can't... I must see...quiet! There is a carriage out there – (*Listens off, while keeping her eyes fixed on the chopping block and the hatchet.*) Don't you think that I can look at blood! Do you think I'm so weak...oh – I'd like to see your blood, your brains on a chopping block – I'd like to see the whole of your sex swimming in a sea like that...I think I could drink from the bowl of your skull, I'd like to bathe my feet in your rib-cage, and I'd like to eat your roasted heart! – You think that I love you; because the fruit of my womb craved your seed; you think I want to bear your progeny beneath my heart and nourish it with my blood – give birth to your child and take your name! Oh, yes, what is your name? I've never heard your surname – you haven't got one, I shouldn't imagine. I'd be called 'Mrs Gatehouse' – or 'Mrs Dungheap' – you dog, wearing my collar, you lackey, with my crest on your buttons – am I to share with my kitchen maid, be a rival to my skivvy! Oh! oh! oh! – You think I'm a coward and want to run away! No, I'm staying now – and let the storm break! My father's coming home...he'll find his desk broken into...his money gone! He'll ring down – on that bell...two rings for the lackey – and then he'll send for the police...and I'll tell them everything!

Everything! Oh, it will be so good to put an end to it –
if only it would end! – And then he'd have a stroke and
die!...Then we'll all be finished – – then there'll be
peace...quiet!... eternal rest! – – – And then the arms
will be smashed against the coffin lid – the noble family
is extinguished – – and the flunkey dynasty continues in
the orphanage...earning its laurels in the gutter and
ending up in prison!

JEAN: It's the royal blood talking now! Good, Miss Julie.
Put the miller back in his sack now!

(*KRISTIN comes in dressed for church with her hymn book
in her hand.*)

MISS JULIE: (*Rushes up to her and falls in her arms as if to
seek protection.*) Help me, Kristin! Save me from this man!

KRISTIN: (*Motionless and cold.*) What kind of spectacle is
this for a Sunday morning! (*Sees the chopping block.*) What
a pigsty! – What's this supposed to mean? And all the
screaming row you're making!

MISS JULIE: Kristin! You're a woman and you are my
friend! Beware of this wretch!

JEAN: (*Rather timid and abashed.*) While you ladies discuss
things, I'll go in and shave! (*Glides out to the right.*)

MISS JULIE: You must understand me; and you must
listen to me!

KRISTIN: No, I frankly don't understand this kind of loose
behaviour! Where are you going dressed up like that in
your travelling clothes – and him standing there with his
hat on – eh? – eh?

MISS JULIE: Listen to me, Kristin; listen to me, and I'll
tell you everything – – –

KRISTIN: I don't want to know...

MISS JULIE: You must listen to me...

KRISTIN: What's it all about? About some foolishness with
Jean! Yes, well, you see I don't care one bit about it,
because it's not my business. But if you're trying to fool
him into doing a bunk, then we'll soon put a stop to that!

MISS JULIE: (*Extremely agitated.*) Please try to be calm now
Kristin and listen to me! I can't stay here and Jean can't
stay here – so we have to go...

KRISTIN: Hm, hm!

MISS JULIE: (*Brightly.*) But do you know what, I've just had an idea – what if we should all three go – abroad – to Switzerland and set up a hotel together. – – I've got some money, you see – – and Jean and I would be responsible for it all – and you, I thought, could do the kitchen...That would be good, wouldn't it! – – – Say yes! Come with us, and then it's all arranged! – – – Say yes then! (*Embraces KRISTIN and strokes her.*)

KRISTIN: (*Cold and thoughtful.*) Hm, hm!

MISS JULIE: (*Presto tempo.*) You've never been travelling, Kristin – you shall see the world. You'd never believe what fun it is to travel on a train – new people all the time – – new countries – and first we'll pass through Hamburg and see the zoological gardens on the way – you'll like that – and then we'll go to the theatre and to hear the opera – and when we get to Munich, there's the museums, you see, and there's Rubens and Raphael, all those great painters as you know – – You must have heard of Munich where Ludwig lived – the king, you see, who went mad. – – And then we'll see his palace – he still has palaces, furnished just like in the fairy tales – and from there it's not far to Switzerland – with the Alps you – imagine the Alps covered with snow right in the middle of summer – and there are oranges growing and laurels that are green all the year round – – –

(*JEAN is visible in the wings right, sharpening his razor on a strop, which he holds in his teeth and his left hand; listens, pleased, to the conversation, nods agreement now and then.*)

(*Tempo prestissimo.*) – And we'd get a hotel there – and I'll sit at reception, while Jean stands there receiving the guests...and go out shopping...write letters – – What a life, believe me – the trains will blow their whistles, the omnibuses will arrive, the bells will ring upstairs, and in the restaurant – – and then I'll write out the bills – and I can salt them you know...You'd never believe how timid the tourists are, when it comes to paying the bill! – And you – you'd be sitting there like the butler in the kitchen. – Of course you wouldn't do any cooking yourself – and

you'd have to be smartly dressed, when people see you –
and you with your looks – – yes I'm not flattering you –
you can catch yourself a husband one fine day! a rich
Englishman, you see – – those people are so easy to –
(*Eases off.*) – catch – – – and then we'll get rich – and
build ourselves a villa by Lake Como – it rains there a
little, sometimes – it's true – but – (*Her talk begins to
abate.*) – the sun is bound to shine too sometimes – – –
even though it looks dark – and – then – otherwise we
could just come home again – and come back – (*Pause.*)
– – here – or somewhere else – – –

KRISTIN: Listen, Miss Julie! Do you believe that yourself?

MISS JULIE: (*Devastated.*) Do I believe it myself?

KRISTIN: Yes!

MISS JULIE: (*Tired.*) I don't know; I don't believe in
anything any more. (*She falls back on to the bench; lays her
head on her arms on the table.*) Nothing! Nothing at all!

KRISTIN: (*Turns to the right where JEAN stands.*) So, you
were thinking of running away!

JEAN: (*Crestfallen, puts his razor down on the table.*) Running
away? That's putting it too strongly! You heard Miss
Julie's plan, and although she's tired now after sitting up,
it's a project that could very well be executed!

KRISTIN: Now you listen to me! Am I meant to cook for
that...

JEAN: (*Sharply.*) Mind your language if you please, when
you speak to your mistress! Do you understand me?

KRISTIN: Mistress!

JEAN: Yes!

KRISTIN: Listen! Listen to it!

JEAN: No, you listen, it might do you some good, and
talk a bit less! Miss Julie is your mistress, and the same
thing you despise her for now, you ought to despise
yourself for!

KRISTIN: I've always had sufficient self-respect to – – –

JEAN: – To be able to despise others! –

KRISTIN: – to never go beneath myself. Try and say that
the Count's cook has gone with the groom or the pig
feeder! Try and say that!

JEAN: Yes, you've been lucky enough to have to do with a decent man!

KRISTIN: Oh yes, a decent man who sells the Count's wheat from the farm – – –

JEAN: You can talk, who takes a percentage from the groceries and backhanders from the butcher!

KRISTIN: What?

JEAN: And you can't have respect for our masters any more! You, you, you!

KRISTIN: Are you coming to church? You may need a good sermon after your exploits!

JEAN: No, I'm not going to church; you can go on your own and confess your doings!

KRISTIN: Yes, I will, and I'll come home with forgiveness, forgiveness enough for both of us! The Saviour has suffered and dies on the cross for all our sins, and if we approach Him with faith and a penitent heart, then He will take our guilt upon Him.

JEAN: Including the groceries?

MISS JULIE: Do you believe that, Kristin?

KRISTIN: It's my living faith, as true as I'm standing here, and it's the faith of my childhood, which I have preserved from my youth, Miss Julie. And where sin abounds, there shall mercy also abound!

MISS JULIE: Oh, if only I had your faith! If only...

KRISTIN: Yes, but you see, you cannot have it, only by God's special grace, and it's not everyone who is granted it – – –

MISS JULIE: Who is granted it then?

KRISTIN: That is the mystery of God's mercy, you see, miss, and God is no respecter of persons, but rather the last shall be first...

MISS JULIE: Yes, but then he shows special consideration for the last?

KRISTIN: (*Continuing.*) – And it is easier for a camel to pass through the eye of a needle than for a rich man to enter the kingdom of Heaven! That's the way it is, Miss Julie! Now I'm going – alone, and incidentally, I'll remind the stable boy not to let any horses out, in case anyone intends to travel, before the Count should return home! – Goodbye! (*Goes.*)

JEAN: What a bitch! – And all this because of a greenfinch! –

MISS JULIE: (*Dully.*) Leave the bird alone! – Do you see any way out of all this, any end?

JEAN: (*Thinks.*) No!

MISS JULIE: What would you do in my place?

JEAN: In your place? Wait now? – As the Count's daughter, as a woman, who's – fallen. I don't know – yes! now I know!

MISS JULIE: (*Picks up the razor and makes a gesture.*) This?

JEAN: Yes! – But *I* wouldn't do it – note! There is a difference between us.

MISS JULIE: Because you are a man and I'm a woman? What difference does that make?

JEAN: The same difference – as that – between men and women!

MISS JULIE: (*Knife in her hand.*) I want to do it! But, I can't! – My father couldn't either, that time he should have done it.

JEAN: No, he shouldn't have done it! He had to have revenge first!

MISS JULIE: And now my mother is having her revenge, through me.

JEAN: Haven't you ever loved your father, Miss Julie?

MISS JULIE: Yes, immensely, but I've hated him too! I must have done without realising! But it's he who brought me up to despise my own sex, as a half woman, half man! Whose fault is it what happened! My father's, my mother's, my own! My own? I have nothing of my own? I don't have a thought that I didn't get from my father, not a passion I didn't get from my mother, and that last – that all people are equal – I got that from him, my fiancé – whom I therefore call wretch! How can it be my own fault? Put the blame over on to Jesus as Kristin does – no, I'm too proud for that and too clever – thanks to my learned father – – – And that a rich man cannot enter Heaven, that's a lie, and Kristin, who has money in the savings bank, won't get there anyway! Whose fault is it? – What do we care whose fault it is! It's still me who has to bear the blame, bear the consequences...

JEAN: Yes, but – – –

(*Two sharp rings of the bell. MISS JULIE stands up; JEAN changes his jacket.*)

The Count is home! What if Kristin – – – (*Goes to the speaking-tube; knocks and listens.*)

MISS JULIE: He's been to his bureau?

JEAN: It's Jean! my lord! (*Listens: the audience doesn't hear the Count speak.*) Yes, my lord! (*Listens.*) Yes, my lord! Straight away! (*Listens.*) At once, my lord! (*Listens.*) Very Good! In half an hour!

MISS JULIE: (*Extremely worried.*) What did he say? Oh Jesus, what did he say?

JEAN: He asked for his boots and his coffee in half an hour.

MISS JULIE: In half an hour then! Oh, I'm so tired; I'm not capable of anything, I can't repent, can't run away, can't stay, can't live – can't die! Help me now! Command me, and I'll obey like a dog! Do me that last service, save my honour, save his name! You know what I *would* want, but don't want...You want it for me, command me to do it!

JEAN: I don't know – but now I can't either – I don't understand – It's just as if this jacket makes me – unable to take command over you – and now, since the Count spoke to me – well – I can't account for it really – but – it's that bloody lackey at my back! – I believe that if the Count came down now – and ordered me to cut my throat, I'd do it on the spot.

MISS JULIE: Then pretend that you are he, and I am you! – you were able to act a part so well just now when you went down on your knees – you were an aristocrat then – or – have you ever been to the theatre and seen a hypnotist? (*Affirmative gesture from JEAN.*) He tells his subject: pick up the broom; he picks it up; sweep: he says, and he sweeps – – –

JEAN: But he has to be asleep!

MISS JULIE: (*Ecstatic.*) I'm already asleep – the whole room is like smoke for me...and you look like an iron stove...which is like a man dressed in black with a high hat – and your eyes are glowing like coals, when the fire is going out – and your face is a white smear like ashes – (*The rays of the sun now fall on the floor and illuminate JEAN.*) – it's so nice and warm – (*She rubs her hands together as if warming them at a fire.*) – and so bright – and so calm!

JEAN: (*Takes up his razor and puts it in her hand.*) There's the broom! Go now while it's light – out into the barn and... (*Whispers in her ear.*)

MISS JULIE: (*Awake.*) Thank you! Now I shall be at peace! But just tell me this – that the first shall also receive the gift of mercy. Say it, even if you don't believe it.

JEAN: The first? No, I can't say that! – But wait – Miss Julie – I know! You are no longer among the first – you are among the – last!

MISS JULIE: That's true. – I am one of the very last; Oh! – But now I can't go – Tell me once more to go!

JEAN: No, now I can't either! I can't!

MISS JULIE: And the first shall be last!

JEAN: Don't think, don't think! You are taking all my strength from me too, making me a coward – – – What! I thought the bell moved! – No! We'll stuff paper in it! – – To be so scared of a bell! – Well, it's not just a bell – there's someone behind it – a hand sets it in motion – and something else sets that hand in motion – just put your hands over your ears – block your ears! yes, but he rings all the more! just rings until you answer – and then it's too late! and then the police will come – and then – – – (*Two loud rings of the bell.*)

JEAN: (*Weakens; then straightens himself.*) It's horrible! But there's no other end to it! – Go! (*MISS JULIE goes resolutely out through the door.*)

The End.

THE COMRADES

Kamraterna

a comedy in five acts

(1888)

Characters

AXEL
a painter

BERTHA
his wife, a painter

ABEL
a friend

WILLMER
a writer

DOCTOR ÖSTERMARK

FRU HALL
His divorced wife

The MISSES HALL
her daughters from a subsequent relationship

CARL STARK
a lieutenant

FRU STARK
wife of Stark

Note on pronunciation of character's names:
AXEL: 'ax-sell'
BERTHA: 'batt-a'
ABEL: 'ah-bell'
WILLMER: 'villmer'
ÖSTERMARK: 'ö' as in french 'oeuf'
HALL: as in french 'mal'

Set for all the acts.

A painter's studio in Paris, on the ground floor, with glass doors to a garden. Upstage a large window, a door to the hall. Sketches, tapestries, weapons, clothes and fragments of plaster models.

To the right a door to the man's room.

To the left a door to the woman's room.

In the centre of the room a little to the left a modelling dais. To the right an easel with equipment.

A sofa. A large stove with transparent gates, through which the glimmering coals can be seen.

A lamp hangs from the ceiling.

ACT ONE

Scene 1

AXEL and the DOCTOR.

AXEL: (*Sitting and painting.*) And you're in Paris too?

DOCTOR: Everything gathers here like at the centre of the world; and you are married? And happy?

AXEL: Oh well, sort of. Yes, I am rather happy. – Of course...

DOCTOR: Of course what?

AXEL: Listen, you're a widower, and you've been married. What was it like being married?

DOCTOR: Very nice...for her!

AXEL: And for you?

DOCTOR: So-so! But you see, one has to compromise, and we did, we compromised, right down the line.

AXEL: And what does it mean to compromise?

DOCTOR: It means: I gave in!

AXEL: You?

DOCTOR: Yes, you wouldn't believe it of a chap like me would you!

AXEL: No, I wouldn't have imagined that! – Listen, you don't believe in women do you?

DOCTOR: No! Of course not! But I love them.

AXEL: In your own way, yes!

DOCTOR: My own way, yes! What is your way?

AXEL: We have an arrangement where we are like friends, you see, and friendship is higher and more enduring than love!

DOCTOR: Hmm! – So Bertha paints as well? Any good?

AXEL: Alright!

DOCTOR: We were good friends once, she and I, that is to say, we always argued a bit. – People are coming. – Shsh! It's Carl and his wife!

AXEL: (*Stands.*) And Bertha not home! Christ!

145

Scene 2

As before. Lieutenant CARL STARK with FRU STARK, come in.

AXEL: So, welcome! We've arranged a meeting from all corners of the globe. Good day, Fru Stark; you look hale and hearty after your journey.

FRU STARK: Thank you, Axel dear, it's been a real pleasure trip for us! But where's Bertha?

CARL: Yes, where's the young wife!

AXEL: She's in her studio; but I'm expecting her home any minute! Won't you sit down!

(*The DOCTOR greets the new arrivals.*)

CARL: Can't really. We just looked in in passing to see where you lived. But we're invited here on Saturday the first of May aren't we?

AXEL: Of course! You got our card then?

FRU STARK: Yes, we received it in Hamburg already! – So, what's Bertha doing these days!

AXEL: Well, she's painting, just like me. We're expecting her model chap to arrive! So I really – I can't invite you to stay, to be honest!

CARL: Do you think we're shy?

FRU STARK: The model isn't...naked surely?

AXEL: Of course!

CARL: A man? My God! – No, I wouldn't let my wife do that. Alone with a naked man?

AXEL: You are still prejudiced Carl!

CARL: Yes, but look...

FRU STARK: Gracious!

DOCTOR: Yes, I quite agree!

AXEL: I can't say that it's to my liking exactly, but as long as I have to have a female model then...

FRU STARK: That's a different matter...

AXEL: Different!

FRU STARK: Yes it *is* different; similar perhaps, but not the same...

(*There is a knock on the door.*)

AXEL: It's him!

FRU STARK: Then we'll go! Goodbye then and *au revoir*!
Say a big hello to Bertha for me!
AXEL: Goodbye then, since you're all so timid. And
au revoir!
CARL/DOCTOR: Goodbye Axel!
CARL: (*To AXEL.*) You will stay here at least?
AXEL: No! What for?
CARL: (*Goes out, shaking his head.*) Ugh!

Scene 3

AXEL alone, painting. There is a knock on the door.

AXEL: Come in!
(*The MODEL comes in.*)
So, here you are again! My wife's not here yet.
MODEL: But it's nearly twelve o'clock, and I've another
appointment afterwards.
AXEL: Well, well! Yes, it is infuriating, but, hmm, there
must have been some delay at the studio. How much do
I owe you?
MODEL: It's five francs as usual!
AXEL: (*Pays him.*) There you are! You can stay a while
anyway.
MODEL: Yes, if I'm needed!
AXEL: Yes, well if you'd sit down for a moment!
(*The MODEL goes behind the screen.*)

Scene 4

AXEL alone. Drawing and whistling. Joined by BERTHA.

AXEL: Well good morning, my dear, so you're home at last?
BERTHA: At last!
AXEL: Yes, the model is waiting!
BERTHA: (*A movement.*) Oh no! no! Has he been here again?
AXEL: You had booked him for eleven o'clock.
BERTHA: Me? No! Did he say that?
AXEL: Yes, but I heard you arrange it yesterday!

147

BERTHA: It's possible, but at any rate, the teacher didn't let us go; you know, it's the last few hours and everyone's nervous. You're not cross with me are you, Axel?

AXEL: Cross? No. But this is the second time, and he still takes the five francs, for nothing!

BERTHA: Can I help it if the teacher keeps us behind. Why do you have to tell me off again? You never...

AXEL: Have I told you off?

BERTHA: What? Well haven't you...

AXEL: Yes, yes, yes, I have told you off! I'm sorry...sorry for thinking it was your fault!

BERTHA: That's alright then! – But, what did you pay him with?

AXEL: Yes, that's a point, I got back the twenty francs Gaga borrowed from me.

BERTHA: (*Takes out a housekeeping book.*) So, you got it back. Let me just write that in! To keep everything in order. It's your money, so naturally you do what you like with it, but since I'm looking after the finances, as you wanted... (*Writes.*) 'Fifteen francs in; five francs out, model.' There.

AXEL: No wait a minute; it was twenty francs in!

BERTHA: Yes, but there's only fifteen here!

AXEL: Yes, but it *was* twenty francs in.

BERTHA: Yes, but there *are* only fifteen in, here, on the table. You can't deny that?

AXEL: No, no, I'm not denying it. There are fifteen francs on the table! There are...

BERTHA: So why are you arguing then?

AXEL: Am I...? – The fellow's waiting.

BERTHA: I see! Set up for me would you!

AXEL: (*Arranges the easel; calls out behind the screen.*) Are you undressed yet?

MODEL: (*Behind the screen.*) In a minute, sir!

BERTHA: (*Closes the door; puts wood in the stove.*) There! You can go now!

AXEL: (*Lingering.*) Bertha!

BERTHA: Yes!

AXEL: Is this all absolutely necessary with the naked model?

BERTHA: It is absolutely necessary!

AXEL: Hmm! I see!

BERTHA: We've already had this argument!

AXEL: That's true! But it's still horrible. (*Goes out right.*)

BERTHA: (*Picks up brushes and palette; calls over towards the screen.*) Are you ready?

MODEL: I'm ready!

BERTHA: Come on then!

(*Pause.*)

Come!

(*A knock on the door.*)

Who is it? I have a model!

WILLMER: (*Outside.*) Willmer! With news from the Salon!

BERTHA: The Salon! (*To the MODEL.*) Get dressed, we'll have to postpone the session! – Axel! Gaga's here with news from the Salon!

(*AXEL comes in; WILLMER; the MODEL goes unnoticed during the following scene.*)

Scene 5

As before. WILLMER.

WILLMER: Good day, dear friends! The jury starts its work this morning. – Here Bertha, the pastels! (*Takes a packet from his pocket.*)

BERTHA: Thanks Gaga! How much were they? Expensive I expect?

WILLMER: Oh, not really!

BERTHA: So, they started this morning already. Hear that Axel?

AXEL: Yes, my friend!

BERTHA: Would you be ever so nice! Ever so!

AXEL: I'm always nice with you, my friend!

BERTHA: Will you? Now listen, you know Roubey don't you?

AXEL: Yes, I met him in Vienna, and you might say we became good friends.

BERTHA: You know he's on the jury.

AXEL: And?

BERTHA: Yes, now you're angry. I knew it!

AXEL: So, you knew it! Then don't make me angry!

BERTHA: (*Strokes him.*) Don't you want to make a sacrifice for your wife!

AXEL: To go and beg? No, I don't!

BERTHA: Not for yourself, because you'll get in anyway, but for your wife!

AXEL: Don't ask me!

BERTHA: I wouldn't normally ask you for anything!

AXEL: Well yes, for things that I can do without sacrificing my...

BERTHA: Your male pride!

AXEL: Oh here we go.

BERTHA: But I would sacrifice my feminine pride, if I could help you.

AXEL: Women have no pride!

BERTHA: Axel!

AXEL: Alright, I'm sorry, I'm sorry!

BERTHA: You are obviously jealous of me! You probably wouldn't like me to get into the Salon.

AXEL: It would give me the greatest pleasure if you got in, believe me Bertha.

BERTHA: Would you still be pleased if I got in and you were rejected?

AXEL: Let me see! (*Puts his hand to his left side.*) It would definitely feel uncomfortable! Definitely! Both because I paint better than you do, and because...

BERTHA: (*Paces about.*) Go on say it, because I am a woman!

AXEL: Yes, for that reason too! It's strange, but it feels as if you would be intruding, marauding, on the field where we had fought while you stood at the stove! Forgive me Bertha for saying it, but these are my thoughts.

BERTHA: Can you see that you are exactly like all other men, exactly!

AXEL: Like all other men! Well, I hope so!

BERTHA: And you've grown so superior lately! You never used to be!

AXEL: That's because I am superior! Try and do something men haven't already done!

BERTHA: What! What are you saying? Aren't you ashamed!

WILLMER: There now, there now, my good friends! Come now, my dear friends! Bertha calm yourself!

(*He gives her a look which she tries to interpret.*)

BERTHA: (*Changing.*) Axel, let's be friends! And listen to me for a moment! Do you think my position in your house – for it *is* yours – is comfortable for me? You support me, pay for my lessons with Julian, while you can't afford to take lessons yourself. Don't you think I can see how you are slaving away and wasting your talent doing these illustrations and only painting in spare moments. Have you even been able to hire a model, while you've been paying for mine at five francs an hour. You don't know yourself how good, how noble, how self-sacrificing you are, but neither do you know how I suffer from watching you slaving for me. Oh, Axel, you can't imagine how it feels in my position. What am I to you? In what capacity am I in your house? Oh, I blush when I think of it!

AXEL: What, what, what! Aren't you my wife?

BERTHA: Yes, but...

AXEL: Well, well?

BERTHA: But, you are supporting me!

AXEL: Well, isn't that what I'm supposed to do?

BERTHA: Before, yes, in old-fashioned marriages it was like that, but we weren't going to be like that! We were going to be friends!

AXEL: What kind of talk is that, shouldn't a man support his wife?

BERTHA: I don't want you to! And you Axel, you must help me. I'm not your equal, while it's like this, but I could be, if you could humble yourself once, just the once! You wouldn't be the only one to go to a juryman and put in a good word for someone else. If it was for yourself, that would be another matter, but for me. For me! Now I'm asking you as nicely as I can. Lift me up

out of my humiliation, to be alongside you, and I shall
be grateful, I shall never torment you any more by
reminding you of my position, never, Axel?

AXEL: Don't ask me, you know how weak I am!

BERTHA: (*Takes him in her arms.*) Yes, I shall ask you, I
shall beg you until you grant my wish! There now, don't
look so proud, be human! There! (*Kisses him.*)

AXEL: (*To WILLMER.*) Do you hear Gaga, don't you think
women are all dreadful tyrants?

WILLMER: (*Troubled.*) Yes, especially when they're being
submissive!

BERTHA: There we are, nice weather again! You will go
now Axel, won't you? There; on with your black coat,
and come back in time for dinner, we'll go out together
and eat.

AXEL: How do you know if Roubey is receiving callers now?

BERTHA: Don't you think I've found out about that?

AXEL: Yes, but you're such a schemer, Bertha!

BERTHA: (*Takes a black frock-coat from the wardrobe.*)
Well, you have to be don't you, otherwise you don't get
anywhere. Here's your black coat! There!

AXEL: Yes, but this is awful. What shall I say to the fellow?

BERTHA: Hmm! You can think of something on your way.
Say that, that, that your wife – no – that you're expecting
a christening...

AXEL: Really Bertha!

BERTHA: Well say, that you can get him a medal!

AXEL: No, you scare me, Bertha!

BERTHA: Say whatever you like then! Come here, let me
do your hair, so you look presentable. Do you know
his wife?

AXEL: Not at all!

BERTHA: (*Brushes his hair, giving him a fringe.*) You should
have yourself introduced to her. She's supposed to have a
lot of influence, but she doesn't like women.

AXEL: What are you up to with my hair?

BERTHA: I'm doing it the way the men are wearing it now.

AXEL: Yes, but I don't like it!

BERTHA: There now! That's better! Do what I tell you now!

(*She goes to the bureau and takes out a case in which lies the order of Russian Annoe[1], which she tries to fasten in his buttonhole.*)

AXEL: No Bertha, you're going too far! I never wear medals!

BERTHA: But you accepted it!

AXEL: Yes, because I couldn't send it back, but I never wear it.

BERTHA: Do you belong to some political party which is so broad-minded as to want to suppress the individual's right to accept honours?

AXEL: No, I don't, but I belong to a circle of friends, who have promised each other not to wear medals on their coats.

BERTHA: But who have accepted awards from the Salon!

AXEL: Which are not worn on the coat!

BERTHA: What do you say to this Gaga!

WILLMER: So long as honours exist, one does oneself a disservice to go about stigmatised, and no one seems to follow the example. Get rid of them, by all means, but you can't stop others getting them.

AXEL: Yes, but when my friends, who are more deserving than I, don't have any, then I belittle them by wearing it.

BERTHA: But when it's not visible under your overcoat, then no one will know, and you won't have stigmatised anyone.

WILLMER: Bertha's right. You wear your medal under your coat, so you're not wearing it *on* your coat.

AXEL: Jesuits! Give you a finger, and take the whole arm.

Scene 6

As before. ABEL comes in; dressed in a fur coat and a fur hat.

BERTHA: Look here's Abel! Come and settle this dispute.

ABEL: Good day Bertha, good day Axel. How are you Gaga? What's the question?

BERTHA: Axel doesn't want to wear his medal, because he doesn't dare to in front of his friends.

[1] During this period a huge variety of honours were awarded by various nations in the form of medallions denoting noble orders.

153

ABEL: Naturally he puts his friends before his wife, it's a law of nature among the masses. (*Sits by a table, takes out her packet of tobacco and starts rolling cigarettes.*)

BERTHA: (*Fastening the ribbon in AXEL's buttonhole and returning the star to its box.*) He could benefit me, without doing anyone any harm, but I'm afraid he would rather harm me!

AXEL: Bertha, Bertha! You'll send me quite mad. I don't consider it to be any crime to wear that ribbon, and I haven't sworn any oath not to do so, but it has long been part of our way of thinking that it is cowardly not to manage to make one's way without.

BERTHA: Unmanly, of course! But you are not making your way this time, you are making mine!

ABEL: You have a symbolic debt, Axel, towards the woman, who has sacrificed her life for you!

AXEL: I feel as if what you are saying is false, but I haven't had the time or the strength, to think out the answer to it! It's as if you are casting a net about me, while I sit buried in my work. I can feel the net closing around me, but my foot gets caught in it when I try to kick it off. Just wait, as soon as I get my hands free, I shall take my knife and cut your net to pieces. – What were we talking about! Ah yes, I was to pay a visit. Right! Give me my gloves and my overcoat! Farewell Bertha! Farewell! – Wait a minute! Where does Roubey live?

WILLMER/ABEL/BERTHA: (*Together.*) Sixty-five Rue des Martyrs!

AXEL: That's just here!

BERTHA: Right here on the corner! Thank you for going, Axel! Does it feel like such a great sacrifice?

AXEL: I feel nothing else except that I am sick of your chatter and it will be a relief to get out of here. Farewell!

Scene 7

WILLMER. ABEL. BERTHA.

ABEL: Poor Axel! It's such a shame! You know that he's been refused!

BERTHA: And me?

ABEL: They haven't decided about you yet; because you wrote your name in the French spelling you come under 'O'.

BERTHA: So there's still hope for me!

ABEL: Yes for you, but not for Axel!

WILLMER: Now we'll see!

BERTHA: How do you know he's been refused?

ABEL: Hmm, I met an *hors concours* who knew about it. And I was rather afraid there might be a scene, when I got here; but he can't have received the notification yet!

BERTHA: No, not as far as I know! But, Abel, are you sure Axel will see Madame Roubey and not Monsieur?

ABEL: Why would he see Monsieur Roubey, he's nothing to do with it, while Madame Roubey is the chairwoman of the Women's Painters Association.

BERTHA: So: I haven't been refused – yet!

ABEL: No, like I say, and Axel's visit is bound to do some good. He has that Russian award and Russia is very popular at the moment in Paris. But it's a pity about Axel though!

BERTHA: A pity! Why! There isn't room for everyone on the walls of the Salon. So many women are refused, let a man see how it feels. But if I do get in, I'm sure we'll hear all about how *he* did my painting, how he's taught me and paid for my lessons. But I shan't pay any attention to that because it isn't true.

WILLMER: Now we shall see something out of the ordinary!

BERTHA: No, I think, presuming I get accepted, that we shall see something quite usual. But I'm still afraid of the moment. Something tells me things aren't going to be very good between Axel and I any more.

ABEL: And it's just when things should be good, when you become equals.

WILLMER: I think both your positions will become much clearer, and yours much more agreeable, when you start selling your work and can support yourself.

BERTHA: Yes it would be! We shall see! We shall see!

Scene 8

As before. The MAID with a green envelope.

BERTHA: A green letter, for Axel! There it is! There it is!
He's been refused! It is terrible though; but it is a
comfort, if it goes badly for me!

ABEL: But if it goes well?

(*BERTHA pauses.*)

You can't answer that?

BERTHA: No, I can't answer that.

ABEL: Because then the equality is disrupted, since you are
on top!

BERTHA: On top! A woman above her husband! Oh!

WILLMER: It's not before time an example was set!

ABEL: You were at the breakfast today? Was it fun?

BERTHA: Oh yes!

WILLMER: Well, when are you going to review my book,
Abel?

ABEL: I'm working on it now!

WILLMER: And will it be a good one?

ABEL: Very good! – Well Bertha and when are you going to
hand over the letter?

BERTHA: That's just what I was wondering! If he hasn't
met Madame Roubey yet, and hasn't carried out his task,
then he's not likely to do it after a blow like this.

ABEL: (*Stands.*) I don't think Axel is so dishonourable as to
take revenge on you.

BERTHA: Dishonourable? Honourable! What's that? Why
did he go just now when I sent him? Because I am *his*
wife. He never would have gone for anyone else!

ABEL: Would you have liked it if he had done it for
someone else?

BERTHA: Farewell you two, you must go now, before he
comes back!

ABEL: Just my thought! Farewell, Bertha!

BERTHA: Now you really must go! *Adieu!*

Scene 9

As before. The MAID announces FRU HALL.

BERTHA: Well, I wonder who this can be?

ABEL/WILLMER: *Adieu* Bertha! (*They go.*)

Scene 10

BERTHA. FRU HALL dressed up, but badly dressed, with a loose appearance.

FRU HALL: I don't know if I have had the honour to be presented to you before! You are Fru Alberg[1], née Ålund[2]?

BERTHA: Yes, that is I, do sit down!

FRU HALL: My name is Hall! Oh my God, I'm so tired, I've walked up so many stairs, dear me! I think I'm going to faint.

BERTHA: How can I be of service?

FRU HALL: Fru Alberg, you know one Doctor Östermark; I believe.

BERTHA: Yes, he's an old friend of mine!

FRU HALL: An old friend, yes! Yes! You see, my dearest Fru Alberg, I used to be married to him, but now we are separated. I am a divorced wife!

BERTHA: Oh! He never told me!

FRU HALL: Well, it's the kind of thing one doesn't tell.

BERTHA: He told me he was a widower.

FRU HALL: Well, you were a young girl then, and I suppose he isn't so eager that it be known.

BERTHA: And I always thought Doctor Östermark was an honourable man.

FRU HALL: Oh yes, he's that all right! A really fine fellow, I can tell you!

BERTHA: But why are you telling me all this?

FRU HALL: Yes, well my dear Fru Alberg, you just wait until you hear this! You are chair of an organisation? Aren't you?

BERTHA: Yes, I am!

[1] Pronounced: 'ahl-barrie' ('g' is soft in Swedish)
[2] Pronounced: 'awe-lund'

FRU HALL: There you are! Just wait until you hear!

BERTHA: Did you have children!

FRU HALL: Two children; two daughters, Fru Ålund!

BERTHA: Then that's another matter! And did he leave you penniless?

FRU HALL: Just wait until you hear this! He threw a miserable amount at me each year, which was never once enough even to pay the rent! And now the girls are grown up and about to go out into the world, he writes to tell me he's penniless, and can't send more than half the usual amount. That's nice isn't it? Just when the girls are grown up and about to go out into the world!

BERTHA: We must do something about this. He's coming here in a couple of days' time. You know, my dear lady, you have the law on your side and the courts can make him pay! And he must be made to pay! Do you hear! I see, so one just brings children into the world and then leaves them helpless with their poor deserted mother! Well, we shall see about that! Would you give me your address?

FRU HALL: (*Hands her a visiting card.*) Dear kind Fru Alberg! You won't be annoyed with me, if I beg of you a little service?

BERTHA: You can depend upon me entirely. I shall at once write to the secretary...

FRU HALL: Oh yes, you are extremely kind, but before the secretary has answered my daughters and I could be thrown on the streets. Good kind Fru Ålund, could you let me have, an insignificant, let me see now! a tiny loan, of say twenty francs.

BERTHA: No, my dear lady, I have no money. My husband is supporting me for the present, and I shan't hear the end of it. It is bitter to taste charity when you are young, but I shall perhaps know better days soon!

FRU HALL: Oh dear, sweet Fru Alberg, don't deny me, or I shall be lost. Help me for heaven's sake!

BERTHA: Are you in great and dire need?

FRU HALL: How can you ask!

BERTHA: You can have this money as a loan. (*She goes to the bureau.*) Twenty, forty, sixty, eighty! Twenty missing. What have I done with it? Hmm! The breakfast! (*Writes in the housekeeping book.*) Paint: twenty; miscellaneous: twenty. – There!

FRU HALL: Thank you dear Fru Ålund, thank you dear lady!

BERTHA: There, there, I haven't any more time for you today. Farewell, and depend on me!

FRU HALL: (*Uncertain.*) Just a minute please!

BERTHA: No, you must go now!

FRU HALL: No, wait please! What was I going to say now? – – – Oh well, it doesn't matter! – (*Goes.*)

Scene 11

BERTHA alone. Then joined by AXEL. BERTHA puts the green envelope in her pocket, when she hears him coming.

BERTHA: Done it already! Well, did you see her – him.

AXEL: I didn't meet him, I met her. And it was just as well. Congratulations Bertha! Your painting has already been accepted!

BERTHA: Oh! No, really? What about yours?

AXEL: That hasn't been decided yet, but I presume that it will also be accepted.

BERTHA: Are you so sure?

AXEL: Naturally…

BERTHA: Oh I've been accepted! What fun, what fun! Well congratulate me then!

AXEL: Didn't I already? I thought I had just congratulated you! Besides, one shouldn't sell the fur before one has shot the bear. Getting into the Salon is nothing. It's just chance! It can depend on what letter your name begins with. You came under 'O', because you spelt your name the French way and since they started at 'M', it went all the better for you.

BERTHA: I see, you're saying that because my name begins with 'O', I got in.

AXEL: Not quite only because of that!

BERTHA: Well, if you are refused, then it's probably because your name begins with 'A'.

AXEL: Not quite only because of that, but to an extent, yes!

BERTHA: Listen, I don't think you're as noble as you make yourself out to be. You're jealous.

AXEL: Why would I be jealous, when I don't know how it went for me yet.

BERTHA: But when you do find out!

AXEL: What!

(*BERTHA takes out the letter.*)

(*Clutches his left side and sits on a chair.*) What! – – –

(*Controls himself.*) That's a blow, that I wasn't expecting. How extremely unpleasant!

BERTHA: Well, I suppose I'll have to help you now!

AXEL: You seem to be gloating, Bertha. Oh I feel a great hatred for you welling up inside me.

BERTHA: If I look pleased, it is perhaps because I have had a success, but if you are tied to a person who can't take pleasure in your success, then it is difficult to feel sympathy for their misfortune.

AXEL: I don't know why, but it seems to me we have become enemies. The battle for status has come between us, we can never be friends again.

BERTHA: Can't your sense of fairness incline to me, seeing that the most able of us has won the field.

AXEL: You are not the most able!

BERTHA: The jury must have thought so at any rate!

AXEL: The jury? But you know you paint less well than I do!

BERTHA: Is that so certain!

AXEL: Well, yes it is! And besides, you were working under more favourable conditions than me. You don't have to do these illustrations, you were able to attend classes, you had models, and you are a woman!

BERTHA: Oh yes, now I suppose I shall hear all about how I have lived off you...

AXEL: Between you and me, yes, but no one need know, unless you go telling people yourself.

BERTHA: Oh, everyone's been told about that already! But tell me, why doesn't it trouble you if a friend, a male friend, gets in though less deserving than you?

AXEL: Let me think now. You see, we have always accepted you women without criticism instinctively, and therefore I've never thought about our attitude towards each other. Now when it comes to the crunch, it seems to me we are not comrades because I can feel as if you have no business here. A friend is more or less a loyal opponent, whereas we are enemies. You've been hiding behind the bushes while we fought the battles, and now we've set the table you come in and make yourselves at home!

BERTHA: Oh God! Have we ever been allowed to join in the fighting?

AXEL: You've always been allowed to, but you haven't wanted to, or been able. In our area where you intrude, the technique had to go through its whole development and be perfected by us, before you arrived. And now you buy the work of a whole century for ten francs an hour in a studio, and with money which we have earnt with our hard work.

BERTHA: Now, at least, you are not noble, Axel!

AXEL: Whenever was I noble? Oh yes, when I allowed you to trample me like an old shoe...but now you stand above me, and I can't bear to be noble any more. Do you know this reverse of mine also changes our economic situation! I can't imagine painting any more, I must abandon my life's ambition, and become an illustrator in earnest.

BERTHA: No you don't; once I start selling, I can support myself.

AXEL: By the way... What kind of association is it we have entered into? Marriage is meant to be built on common interests, ours is built on conflicting ones.

BERTHA: You'll have to work that out by yourself; I'm going out to eat dinner; are you coming?

AXEL: No, I want to be alone in my misery.

BERTHA: And I must have company in my happiness. – – – Oh yes, we've invited people here this evening to your house! That won't do, now you have your bereavement.

AXEL: It's no fun, but it will have to go ahead. Let them come!

BERTHA: (*Gets dressed to go out.*) But you must be here, otherwise it would look as if you were in a funk.

AXEL: I shall be here, don't worry! – But can you give me a bit of money before you go.

BERTHA: There isn't any left in the pot.

AXEL: None left?

BERTHA: Yes, money does run out, you know.

AXEL: Can you lend me ten francs?

BERTHA: (*Takes out her purse.*) Ten francs. I see! If I've got it! – Here you are! – Won't you come? Go on! People will think it so strange if you don't!

AXEL: And play the conquered lion in your triumph! No thanks! I need some time to learn my new role for this afternoon's performance.

BERTHA: *Adieu* then!

AXEL: *Adieu*! Bertha! May I ask you one thing!

BERTHA: What is it?

AXEL: Don't come home drunk! It would be especially unpleasant today!

BERTHA: What business is it of yours, how I come home.

AXEL: Well, I feel a kind of solidarity with you, as I would with a relation, since we bear the same name, and besides I find it disgusting to see a woman drunk.

BERTHA: Why is it more disgusting than seeing a man drunk?

AXEL: Yes, why? Perhaps because you can't bear to be seen without making a performance.

BERTHA: *Adieu*, you old gasbag! – You aren't coming? (*Goes.*)

AXEL: (*Stands up, and takes off his frock-coat in order to change his jacket.*) No!

End of Act One.

ACT TWO

Same set as before. A large table with chairs around it in the centre of the room; on the table, writing materials, paper, and a chairman's gavel.

Scene 1

AXEL sitting painting. ABEL next to him on a chair smoking.

AXEL: So, they've finished eating and they're on the coffee now? Did they drink much?

ABEL: Oh yes! Bertha was bragging and being unpleasant.

AXEL: Tell me something, Abel, are you my friend or aren't you?

ABEL: We-ell, I don't know about that.

AXEL: Can I trust you?

ABEL: No, you can't.

AXEL: Why's that?

ABEL: I think it feels as if you can't.

AXEL: Listen Abel, you've got a man's common sense and one can reason with you, listen, tell me what is it like to be a woman! Is it so terrible?

ABEL: (*Jesting.*) Yes, naturally! It's like being a nigger.

AXEL: That's extraordinary. Listen Abel – You know I have a passion for fairness and justice.

ABEL: I know you're a dreamer – – and consequently things never go well for you.

AXEL: But things go well for you – – because you feel nothing?

ABEL: Yes.

AXEL: Abel, have you really no need to love a man?

ABEL: How silly you are!

AXEL: Have you never found anyone?

ABEL: No. There are so few men.

AXEL: Well, don't you think I am a man?

ABEL: You! – No!

AXEL: I imagine that I am.

ABEL: Are you a man! You work for a woman, and dress as a woman.

AXEL: Me, dress as a woman!

ABEL: You've got a fringe and you don't wear a tie; while she wears a choker and has a page-boy cut; watch out; she'll soon have the trousers off you!

AXEL: The way you talk!

ABEL: And what position do you have in your house? You beg money from her and she puts you in tutelage. No, you're no man! But that's why she took you, when her own affairs were in disorder.

AXEL: You hate Bertha; what have you got against her!

ABEL: I don't know, but perhaps I too have a touch of that passion for justice?

AXEL: Come now, don't you believe in your great cause!

ABEL: Sometimes! Sometimes not! What is one to believe in these days! Sometimes it seems to me that the old way was the most favourable. As mothers we had a respected and honoured position, in which we fulfilled our duty as citizens; as housewives we were the absolute rulers, and bringing up the family was no dishonourable occupation. Give me a cognac, Axel! We've talked too much!

AXEL: (*Takes out the cognac.*) Why do you drink?

ABEL: I don't know! I suppose I'm stale. (*Drinks.*) Oh, to see a marvel before I die!

AXEL: What would that be?

ABEL: That would be a man who could master a woman!

AXEL: Well, and if you did get to see one?

ABEL: Then I would – what do you call it – love him! Imagine if it were just *une blague* the whole palaver! Imagine!

AXEL: No, there is some kind of movement there, whatever kind of movement that may be!

ABEL: Yes, there's such a lot of movement backwards and forwards. – And folly can be put into motion as long as there is a majority in favour of it!

AXEL: If that's the case, then you women have made the devil of a row for nothing, because life is really becoming unpleasant.

ABEL: We make such a row that you become dizzy! That's
the thing. – Well Axel, you'll have an easier position in
this household, now Bertha has begun to sell!

AXEL: Sell! Has she sold something?

ABEL: Don't you know? That little painting of the apple
tree!

AXEL: No, she hasn't told me about that! When was it?

ABEL: The day before yesterday! Don't you know? Well,
then she intends to surprise you with the money.

AXEL: Me? She runs the household herself!

ABEL: So! Then it must be... Shsh, here she comes!

Scene 2

As before. BERTHA.

BERTHA: (*To ABEL.*) Well hello, here you are. Why did
you leave?

ABEL: I thought it was boring!

BERTHA: Yes, it's no fun rejoicing with others.

ABEL: No!

BERTHA: And you sit here painting so diligently Axel!

AXEL: Yes, I'm sitting here fiddling about.

BERTHA: Can I see! Yes, it's good, but the left arm is
too long!

AXEL: Do you think so?

BERTHA: Think so? I can see that it is! Here... (*Takes his
brush from him.*)

AXEL: Leave off! Aren't you ashamed!

BERTHA: What did you say!

AXEL: (*Angry.*) Ashamed, I said! (*Stands up.*) Are you trying
to teach me to paint?

BERTHA: Why not?

AXEL: Because you can learn from me, but I can learn
nothing from you.

BERTHA: I think the gentleman is treating his wife with a
lack of respect. He ought to know with what respect one
should...

ABEL: Now you are being old-fashioned, Bertha! What special respect is due to women, when they're supposed to be equals?

BERTHA: I see, so you think it is right for a man to be coarse with his wife?

ABEL: Yes, when she is rude to him!

AXEL: That's right! Tear each other's eyes out!

ABEL: Oh no, it's too slight a matter for that!

AXEL: I wouldn't say that! – Listen, Bertha. Since our finances from now on are going to undergo some changes, I would like to know how they stand. May I see the housekeeping book!

BERTHA: That's a noble revenge for being refused by the Salon!

AXEL: What revenge! What is the connection between the housekeeping book and my bad luck at the Salon? Give me the key to the bureau!

BERTHA: (*Looks for the key in her pocket.*) Here you are! – Hmm! That's peculiar, I thought I had it just now!

AXEL: Look for it!

BERTHA: You speak in such a commanding tone! I don't like it!

AXEL: Find the key!

BERTHA: (*Searches the room.*) But this is inexplicable! – It's gone! I can't find it. It must be lost!

AXEL: Are you sure it isn't anywhere?

BERTHA: Completely sure!

(*AXEL talks into the speaking tube.*)

(*Pause.*)

Scene 3

As before. The MAID comes in.

AXEL: Fetch a locksmith!

MAID: A locksmith!

AXEL: A locksmith to break open a lock!

MAID: (*Casts a glance at BERTHA.*) At once! (*Goes.*)

Scene 4

As before without the MAID.

AXEL: (*Changes his coat; takes off the medal ribbon and throws it on the floor.*) Excuse me ladies!
BERTHA: (*Gently.*) Don't mind us! Are you going out?
AXEL: I'm going out!
BERTHA: Aren't you staying for the meeting?
AXEL: No, I'm not!
BERTHA: People will think it very discourteous!
AXEL: Let them! I've got better things to do than listen to your drivel.
BERTHA: (*Worried.*) Where will you go?
AXEL: I don't have to render account to you, I don't ask you where you're going!
BERTHA: You won't forget that we've invited the carnival people tomorrow evening.
AXEL: Have we? So we have. Tomorrow evening. Hmm!
BERTHA: We can't cancel it, Östermark and Carl were here today and I asked them to come too.
AXEL: All the better!
BERTHA: So be home in good time so you can try on your suit.
AXEL: My suit! Of course. I'm to play the woman.

Scene 5

As before. The MAID.

MAID: The locksmith hasn't got time now, but he'll come in a couple of hours.
AXEL: He hasn't time! – Well! – Perhaps the key will turn up anyway! Now I must go. *Adieu!*
BERTHA: (*Softly.*) *Adieu* then! Don't be late!
    (*ABEL nods farewell to AXEL.*)
AXEL: I don't know if I shall be or not. *Adieu!* (*Goes.*)

Scene 6

ABEL and BERTHA.

ABEL: How self-assured your husband was!

BERTHA: How rude! You know I'd like to crush him, and see him come crawling after me.

ABEL: Yes, getting burnt over that business with the Salon doesn't seem to have been enough for him. – Bertha, tell me: have you ever loved that idiot?

BERTHA: Loved him? – I liked him very much because he was kind. But he is stupid and…when he gets troublesome, then I really feel as if I could hate him. Imagine, word is already out that he did my painting.

ABEL: If it's gone that far, you'll have to do something spectacular.

BERTHA: If only I knew how?

ABEL: I'm normally inventive. Let me see now! I know! If you should collect his rejected painting tomorrow evening, and have it arrive while the guests are here.

BERTHA: No, that would seem as if I wanted to gloat. It's too cruel.

ABEL: Well, if I arrange it then! Or Gaga, even better. The concierge can send for it in Axel's name. It has to come back anyway, and it's no secret that it's been returned.

BERTHA: No, look…

ABEL: What? He's spreading false rumours, and you've a right to defend yourself!

BERTHA: I'd really like it to happen, but I don't want to have anything to do with it. I want to be able to remain spotless and be able to swear my innocence.

ABEL: You shall be! I'll take care of it!

BERTHA: What do you think he wants the housekeeping book for? He's never asked for it before! Is he plotting something?

ABEL: Oh yes! Something like that I expect! He wants to see if you've written up those three hundred francs you got for your painting under your income.

BERTHA: What painting?

ABEL: The one you sold to Madame Roubey.

BERTHA: How do you know about that?

ABEL: The whole world knows about that!

BERTHA: And Axel too?

ABEL: Yes, I happened to tell him, because I thought he knew. It was terribly stupid of you not to tell him about it at once.

BERTHA: Is it his business if I sell something!

ABEL: Well, yes in a way! I suppose it is!

BERTHA: Well then, in that case I shall say that I didn't want to upset him further, since he already had the great sorrow of me getting into the Salon.

ABEL: Strictly speaking your income is nothing to do with him, since you have a special arrangement in your marriage, and you have every reason to be frugal with him, if only to set an example. Stick to your guns, when he starts lecturing you this evening!

BERTHA: Oh I think I know how to deal with him! But – one more thing. How shall we deal with this Östermark business?

ABEL: Östermark, yes, my great enemy! Let me take care of him! We've some old scores to settle, he and I. Don't you worry! We'll get the better of him, for we have the law on our side!

BERTHA: What do you intend to do?

ABEL: We shall confront the two parties, as they say.

BERTHA: What does that mean?

ABEL: Invite Fru Hall here with her two daughters, see how that will make him look!

BERTHA: No, no scandal in my house!

ABEL: Why not? Can you deny yourself such a triumph. If it's war, you have to kill your enemies, and not just wound them. And this is war. So!

BERTHA: Yes, but a father and his wife and daughters, whom he hasn't seen for eighteen years.

ABEL: Well, he can see them now.

BERTHA: You're dreadful, Abel!

ABEL: I am a little stronger than you. Marriage must have softened you up! You do live as married, don't you?

BERTHA: Don't be silly!

ABEL: You've vexed Axel; you've trampled on him, but he can still bite your heel! So!

BERTHA: Do you think he'd dare do anything?

ABEL: I think there'll be a scene when he comes home!

BERTHA: Ah, I shall give as good as I get!

ABEL: Can you though! That business with the key to your desk was stupid. Very stupid!

BERTHA: Maybe it was stupid. But he'll calm down once he's been out and got some fresh air. I know him.

Scene 7

As before. The MAID comes in with a bundle.

MAID: There's a delivery man here with a suit for the master!

BERTHA: Aha! Give it here! That's fine!

MAID: But it must be for you madam, it's ladies' clothes.

BERTHA: No, it's quite right! It's for the master.

MAID: Strike me, is he going to wear skirts now and all!

BERTHA: Why not, we wear them. Off you go now! (*Opens the parcel and takes out a Spanish dress.*)

ABEL: Oh yes, but that's a perfect idea. How sweet to get revenge on that idiot.

Scene 8

As before. WILLMER with a messenger carrying two packets.

WILLMER: (*Dressed in black evening dress with white shirt cuffs; a flower in his lapel; plus-fours; red cravat; and pleated cuffs.*) Good evening, all alone! Here are the candles, and here's the wine. A Chartreuse and a Vermouth; and here are a couple of packets of tobacco and that other thing.

BERTHA: You are a nice boy, Gaga!

WILLMER: And here's the bill paid!

BERTHA: It's been paid! So you've paid out again!

WILLMER: Yes, we can sort it out another time. But hurry up now, the old woman will be here soon.

BERTHA: Would you be a good boy and open the bottles, while I light the candles.

WILLMER: I certainly will!

(*BERTHA opens the packet of candles by the table; WILLMER stands next to her and unwraps the bottles.*)

ABEL: What a nice domestic scene. You'd have made a nice little husband Gaga.

(*WILLMER puts his hand on BERTHA's throat and kisses her neck.*)

BERTHA: (*Turns and slaps his face.*) Shame on you, you rascal! What do you think you're doing?

ABEL: If you put up with that Gaga, you'll put up with anything.

WILLMER: (*Enraged.*) Rascal? Don't you know who I am! Don't you know I am a writer of rank!

BERTHA: You; with that trash you write!

WILLMER: It wasn't trash, when I wrote for you.

BERTHA: You just wrote up what we said, that's all!

WILLMER: Be careful Bertha; you know I can bring you down.

BERTHA: I see, is that a threat, you little scoundrel. Shall we take him and fry him, Abel!

ABEL: Bertha, think what you're saying!

WILLMER: I see, so I've been a little scoundrel in your wake have I; but I can bite too!

BERTHA: Let's see your teeth then!

WILLMER: No, you shall feel them!

BERTHA: Oh yes! Come on then! Come on!

ABEL: There there, calm yourselves now, before you regret it!

WILLMER: (*To BERTHA.*) Do you know what one can call a married woman, who accepts gifts from a young man?

BERTHA: Gifts!

WILLMER: For two years you've accepted gifts from me.

BERTHA: Gifts! You should be whipped, you treacherous insect, always hanging onto my apron strings. Don't you think I can take care of you!

WILLMER: (*With a shrug of the shoulders.*) Yes, possibly.

BERTHA: How dare you cast aspersions on a lady's honour.

WILLMER: Honour! Hmm! Is it honourable that I should buy things for your household, which you then charge to your husband's account.

BERTHA: Get out of my house, you wretch!

WILLMER: Your house! With friends one doesn't split hairs, but with enemies it pays to reckon them all! And you shall have to reckon with me – adventuress! Depend upon it! (*Goes.*)

Scene 9

BERTHA. ABEL.

ABEL: Your stupidity will be your downfall, Bertha! To let a friend part as an enemy, it's dangerous.

BERTHA: Oh, let him do his worst! He dared to kiss me! He dared to remind me I am a woman.

ABEL: You know, I think men will always remember that! You played with fire.

BERTHA: Fire! A man and a woman can never live together without there being fire.

ABEL: No, well, as long as there are two sexes, there will always be flames!

BERTHA: Yes, but it shall be extinguished!

ABEL: Yes – that's right…Try it!

Scene 10

As before. The MAID.

MAID: (*Holding back her laughter.*) There's a lady outside, calling herself…Richard…Richard Wahlström[1]!

BERTHA: (*Goes to the door.*) Oh, Richard is here!

ABEL: Well, then we can let the meeting begin! – Let's see if we can unravel this mess, Bertha!

BERTHA: Unravel it or just cut it off!

ABEL: Or get caught up in it!

End of Act Two.

[1] Pronounced: 'varl-strurm'

ACT THREE

Same set as before. The ceiling lamp is lit. Moonlight outside the studio window. The stove is alight.

Scene 1

BERTHA and the MAID. BERTHA dressed in a lace dressing gown, is stitching the Spanish dress; the MAID is making a pleat.

BERTHA: It's no fun waiting up for one's husband.

MAID: Does madam think it's any more fun for your husband waiting up for his wife. This is the first time he's gone out on his own...

BERTHA: Well, what does he do, while he's sitting at home on his own?

MAID: He sits painting on logs!

BERTHA: Logs!

MAID: Yes, he's got big piles of wood that he paints on.

BERTHA: Hmm! Tell me Ida. Has he ever made advances to you!

MAID: Never! No, he's a decent man!

BERTHA: Are you sure?

MAID: (*Completely sure.*) Does madam think, I'm the type of girl...

BERTHA: What time is it?

MAID: About twelve o'clock.

BERTHA: Well! You can go to bed now.

MAID: Isn't madam afraid of the dark with all these skeletons around!

BERTHA: Me, afraid of the dark! – Shsh, that was the front door! There, goodnight now!

MAID: Goodnight madam! Sleep well! (*Goes.*)

Scene 2

BERTHA alone: puts down her sewing; throws herself upon the sofa; arranges the lace on her dressing gown. Then she jumps up:

turns down the lamp to about half, resumes her position on the sofa and pretends to sleep. A pause: then AXEL comes in.

AXEL: Is anyone there? – Is that you Bertha?
(*BERTHA is silent.*)
AXEL: (*Goes up to her.*) Are you asleep?
BERTHA: (*Softly.*) Oh! It's you my friend! Hello! I must have dropped off, and I was having such horrible dreams...
AXEL: You're lying, I saw you through the window from the courtyard, taking up your position on the sofa.
(*BERTHA jumps up.*)
(*Calmly.*) No seduction scenes in your nightgown! No melodramas! Calm down and listen to what I've got to tell you! (*Sits on a chair in the centre of the room.*)
BERTHA: What have you got to tell me?
AXEL: A great deal; but I shall begin at the end: we must dissolve this concubinage.
BERTHA: What? (*Throws herself back upon the sofa.*) Oh my God, what shall I have to endure next.
AXEL: Don't get hysterical, or I'll smash the water jug on your lace!
BERTHA: This is your revenge for me defeating you, in open contest.
AXEL: It has nothing whatsoever to do with it!
BERTHA: You have never loved me!
AXEL: Yes, I have loved you, it was my only reason for marrying you; but why did you marry me? Because you had poor finances and anaemia!
BERTHA: It's just as well no-one can hear us!
AXEL: It wouldn't matter if someone heard us. I have treated you like a friend, with unlimited trust, and I have even made small sacrifices, as you know. – Has the locksmith been?
BERTHA: No, he didn't turn up!
AXEL: We don't need him anyway. I've read your accounts.
BERTHA: I see, you go snooping around in my books.
AXEL: The housekeeping book is common to both of us! You've entered false outgoings, and omitted to put down certain incomes.

BERTHA: Yes well, they don't teach us book-keeping at school.

AXEL: They don't teach us either! And as far as upbringing is concerned, you've had better than I: you went to a seminary, but I just went to elementary school.

BERTHA: It's not books that make an upbringing...

AXEL: No, it's the mother! But oddly enough mothers aren't able to teach their daughters to be honest...

BERTHA: Honest! I wonder now, are not most criminals men?

AXEL: The ones that are punished, you mean, but behind ninety-nine per cent of all criminals one may ask along with the judge *où est la femme?* – But – to get back to you. – You have lied to me all the way along, and in the end betrayed me. Here for example it says twenty francs for paint instead of twenty francs for breakfast at Marguery's.

BERTHA: That's not true; it only cost twelve francs.

AXEL: So you pocketed eight francs! – And you never mentioned the three hundred francs you got for the painting you sold.

BERTHA: 'What the woman earns through her own work she may dispose of herself', it says so in the law!

AXEL: There's no paradox there? No monomania!

BERTHA: No, there doesn't seem to be!

AXEL: Well, let's not be petty about it, you dispose of what is yours and also mine, in a quite indefensible way. Don't you think though – between friends – that you ought to have told me you'd sold a painting?

BERTHA: It didn't concern you.

AXEL: It didn't concern me! Well, all that remains then is for me to sue for a divorce.

BERTHA: Divorce! Do you think I intend to bear the disgrace of being a divorced wife! Do you think I'd let you drive me out of my home, like a maid sent away with her trunk!

AXEL: I could have you thrown out onto the street, if I wanted, but I shall take the humane approach and seek a divorce on grounds of incompatibility!

BERTHA: If you can talk like this, then you've never loved me!

AXEL: Answer me this; why did I beg for your hand?

BERTHA: Because you wanted me to love you.

AXEL: Oh holy, inviolable, venerated stupidity! – I could accuse you of forgery, for running up a debt with Willmer and passing it on to me.

BERTHA: Aha, so that little insect has been up to his tricks.

AXEL: I've just come from him after having paid him three hundred and fifty francs, which *you* owed him. But we shan't be petty over the money issue. We have worse business to sort out. You have allowed this whelp to subsidise my household, and by doing so completely destroyed my reputation. What have you done with the money?

BERTHA: Everything you're saying is lies!

AXEL: You've wasted it on parties?

BERTHA: No, I've saved it; something you know nothing about, squanderer!

AXEL: Oh, you thrifty soul you! That dressing gown there cost two hundred francs and mine cost twenty-five.

BERTHA: Have you anything else to say?

AXEL: Nothing other than that you had better think about how you are going to support yourself henceforward. I don't want to carry on drawing on logs of wood while you accumulate the profits.

BERTHA: I see, you think it's that easy to walk away from the responsibilities you assumed, when you fooled me into becoming your wife. We shall see!

AXEL: Now my eyes are opened past events are beginning to take on a different complexion. It seems to me now as if you evoked my proposal of marriage; it occurs to me almost as if I have occasionally been the victim of what you would call seduction; it seems to me these days as if I have fallen into the hands of an adventuress, who wants to cheat me out of my money in a rented room; it seems to me almost as if I have lived in vice, since I joined myself to you! (*Stands up.*) When you stand there like

that with your back to me and I can see your neck and
your short hair, it's as if – – – yes it's just as if – ugh! as if
you were Judith and you've let me have your body so
that you can take off my head. Look, there's the dress,
which I was to wear, which you were to humiliate me
with! Yes, because you thought it was demeaning to wear
these broad pleats which hide in order to tease, the low-
cut bodice, which on the corset's two plates serves up the
dish. No! Here, you can take back your wages of love,
I'm breaking my chains! (*Throws down his wedding ring.*)
(*BERTHA looks at him in wonderment.*)
(*Sweeps back his hair.*) You didn't dare see that I had a
higher forehead than you, and so I allowed my hair to
conceal it, so as not to humiliate and frighten you! But
you see, now I shall humiliate you, and since you can't
content yourself with being my equal when I lowered
myself, you shall have to be my inferior, which you are!

BERTHA: All this, all this noble revenge, just because you
were inferior to me!

AXEL: I was superior to you even while I did your painting!

BERTHA: You did my painting? Say that again, and I shall
hit you!

AXEL: You who so despise brute force, are always the first
to resort to it! Go on hit me!

BERTHA: Don't you think I can? (*She goes towards him.*)

AXEL: (*Takes both her wrists in one hand and holds them fast.*)
No, I don't think so! Are you convinced now that I am
also physically superior! Bend, or I shall break you!

BERTHA: Do you dare to hit me?

AXEL: Why not? I know of only one reason why I shouldn't
hit you.

BERTHA: And that is?

AXEL: Your incapacity.

BERTHA: (*Tries to get loose.*) Oh, let me go!

AXEL: When you've asked for forgiveness! So, on your
knees! (*He forces her to her knees with one hand.*) Look up
to me now, from below! That is your place, which you
have chosen yourself!

BERTHA: (*Gives in.*) Axel, Axel! I don't recognise you any more! Are you the one who swore to love me, to support me, to raise me up.

AXEL: It is I! I was strong then and believed I had the strength to do it, but you cut off my hair, while I lay my tired head on your lap, you sucked out my best blood in my sleep – and still I had enough left to subdue you. Stand up and let's stop declaiming. We've business to discuss!
(*BERTHA gets up; sits on the sofa crying.*)
Why are you crying?

BERTHA: I don't know! Maybe because I'm weak!
(*BERTHA in silent show all the time: indicating her transition.*)

AXEL: You see, your strength, that was me! When I took it back, you had none left. You were like a rubber ball, which I had inflated; when I let go, you collapsed like an empty sack.

BERTHA: (*Without looking up.*) I don't know if it is like you say, but since we've been quarrelling my strength has left me! Axel, if you can believe me, I have never felt like I do now about you!

AXEL: So, what do you feel?

BERTHA: I can't say! I don't know if it's...love, but...

AXEL: What do you mean by love! Isn't it an inexorable desire to eat me alive once again. You're beginning to love me! Why not before, when I was good to you! Goodness is stupidity, let's be nasty! That's it isn't it?

BERTHA: Yes, rather be a bit nasty, than weak. (*Gets up.*) Axel, forgive me, but don't abandon me. Love me! Oh, love me!

AXEL: It's too late! Yesterday, this morning I would have fallen for you, as you stand before me now, but now it's too late!

BERTHA: Why is it too late now?

AXEL: Because tonight I have broken all ties, even the last one!

BERTHA: (*Takes his hands.*) What do you mean?

AXEL: I have been unfaithful!

BERTHA: (*Collapses.*) Oh!

AXEL: It was the only way to break free!

BERTHA: (*Recovers.*) Who was she?

AXEL: A woman...

(*Pause.*)

BERTHA: What did she look like?

AXEL: Like a woman! With long hair, high chest, etcetera!
Spare yourself!

BERTHA: Do you think I'm jealous, of – one of those!

AXEL: One of those, two of those, many of those!

BERTHA: (*Catches her breath.*) And tomorrow our friends
are invited. Will you cause a scandal and cancel it?

AXEL: No, I don't want to be low in my revenge!
Tomorrow we hold the party, and the day after, we go
our separate ways!

BERTHA: Yes, now our ways must part! – Goodnight!
(*Goes to the door left.*)

AXEL: Goodnight! (*Goes to the door right.*)

BERTHA: (*Stops.*) Axel!

AXEL: Yes!

BERTHA: No, nothing! – Yes, wait! (*Goes to him with hands
clasped.*) Love me; Axel! Love me!

AXEL: Do you want to share with another?

BERTHA: (*Pause.*) Yes! If only you love me!

AXEL: No, I can't. You don't attract like you did before!

BERTHA: Love me, out of pity! I'm being truthful now,
I think, for otherwise I would never demean myself like
this, like I am, before a man.

AXEL: Even if I had sympathy for you, I couldn't order
myself to love you. It's finished, it's dead!

BERTHA: I am begging for a man's love, I, a woman, and
he pushes me away!

AXEL: Why not! We can say no too sometimes, can't we,
even if we're not so fussy.

BERTHA: A woman offering herself to a man and being
told no!

AXEL: See how millions have felt, begging on their knees
to be allowed to give what the other receives! Look for
the whole of your sex and then go and tell them how
it feels!

BERTHA: (*Stands.*) Goodnight! So the day after tomorrow!
AXEL: And you still want the party tomorrow?
BERTHA: Yes, I still want the party tomorrow!
AXEL: Fine! So – the day after tomorrow!
   (*They both go off their separate ways as before.*)

   End of Act Three.

ACT FOUR

Same set as before. Except that the French windows are open. The sun is shining outside and the studio is brightly lit. The side doors to the room stand open. In the garden can be seen a buffet table with glasses and bottles etc.

AXEL is dressed in a black frock-coat without his medal; his collar is up and he wears a long cravat, his hair is swept back. BERTHA: in a dark dress, with square neckline, with scarf and frills. She wears a flower on her left shoulder. CARL: wears civilian clothes with medals. The MISSES HALL, are extravagantly and expensively dressed.

Scene 1

BERTHA comes in from the garden. She is pale with blue shadows around her eyes. ABEL comes in from the upstage door. They embrace and kiss.

BERTHA: Good day, welcome! You're late!

ABEL: Good day.

BERTHA: And Gaga has promised to come!

ABEL: Definitely. He's full of remorse and begs your forgiveness.

(*BERTHA adjusts her frills.*)

ABEL: What's the matter with you today? There is something.

BERTHA: What? What did you say?

ABEL: You're not yourself! You've... Bertha! You've...

BERTHA: Oh stop it!

ABEL: You've some colour in your cheeks; there's a light in your eye! What? And so pale? Bertha!

BERTHA: I must go outside to my guests.

ABEL: Tell me, is Carl here, and Östermark?

BERTHA: The two of them are out in the garden.

ABEL: And the Hall girls, and Fru Hall?

BERTHA: Fru Hall is coming later, but the girls are here, in my room.

ABEL: I suppose this is going to be a flop as well.

BERTHA: Oh no it isn't, not this!

Scene 2

As before. WILLMER with a bunch of flowers. Goes up to BERTHA,
kisses her hand and gives her the bouquet.

WILLMER: Forgive me! For the sake of my love!
BERTHA: No, not for that, but – it doesn't matter! I don't
know – but today I don't want any enemies!

Scene 3

As before. AXEL.

BERTHA and WILLMER embarrassed.

AXEL: (*To BERTHA, ignoring WILLMER.*) I'm sorry! If I'm
interrupting!
BERTHA: Not at all!
AXEL: I just wanted to know if you have ordered supper?
BERTHA: Of course. As you wished!
AXEL: Right, I just wanted to know!
ABEL: How solemn you both look!
(*BERTHA and AXEL. WILLMER goes out into the garden.*)
ABEL: Hey! Gaga! (*She rushes after him.*)

Scene 4

BERTHA and AXEL.

AXEL: What have you ordered for supper?
BERTHA: (*Looks at him and smiles.*) Lobster and chicken.
AXEL: (*Uncertain.*) What are you smiling at?
BERTHA: At what you're thinking.
AXEL: What am I thinking?
BERTHA: You're thinking – oh well, of course I don't know
– unless you're thinking about that first dinner we had
together as an engaged couple at Djurgården[1], that spring
evening when you had proposed...
AXEL: When *you* had proposed...
BERTHA: Axel! – And now it's our last; the last time.
It was a short summer!

[1] Pronounced: 'you-r-gore-den'

182

AXEL: Too short; but the sun will come again.

BERTHA: Yes for you, since you find sunshine on every street corner.

AXEL: What's to stop you finding warmth at the same fire.

BERTHA: So we might meet again, do you mean, in the lamplight?

AXEL: I didn't mean that...but *à la bonne heure*! At least it will be an open relationship.

BERTHA: Yes very open; particularly for you.

AXEL: For you too. But more pleasant for me.

BERTHA: What a noble thought.

AXEL: There there – – don't open old wounds! We were talking about supper! And we mustn't forget our guests! Right! (*Goes to his room.*)

BERTHA: Supper! Yes, of course! That's what we were supposed to be talking about. (*Goes to her room, upset.*)

Scene 5

The MISSES HALL come in from the garden. Then DOCTOR ÖSTERMARK.

MISS AMELIE: Boring here isn't it?

MISS THERESE: I think it's unbearable. And our hosts aren't quite polite.

MISS AMELIE: I think she's particularly unpleasant. She's one of those with the page boy-haircut!

MISS THERESE: Yes but there is supposed to be a lieutenant coming...

MISS AMELIE: Well, good, because these artists are, what-do-you-call-it, freetraders. Shsh, now this one must be a diplomat...he looks so distinguished.

(*They sit on the sofa.*)

DOCTOR: (*From the garden, regarding them through his pince nez.*) I'm honoured ladies! Hmm! One meets so many of one's countrywomen here. You ladies are also artists? You paint I expect?

MISS AMELIE: No, we don't paint!

DOCTOR: Oh a little surely! Here in Paris all the ladies paint – themselves.

MISS THERESE: We don't need to.

DOCTOR: Do you play then?

MISS AMELIE: Play?

DOCTOR: Yes, play cards I mean! All ladies play a little.

MISS AMELIE: You must have arrived recently from the country, my good sir.

DOCTOR: Oh yes, quite recently, miss. Can I be of any service?

MISS THERESE: I'm sorry, we don't know whom we have the honour of addressing?

DOCTOR: You ladies must have arrived recently from Stockholm. In this country we dare to speak to one another without asking guarantees.

MISS THERESE: We haven't asked for any guarantee.

DOCTOR: What are you asking for then? To have your curiosity satisfied. Well, I'm an old family doctor and my name is Andersson. Perhaps I might know your names – – Your titles I don't need.

MISS THERESE: We are the Misses Hall, if that is of any interest to you.

DOCTOR: Hall? Hmm! I'm sure I've heard that name before. Forgive me, forgive me a question? A somewhat rustic question?

MISS THERESE: Don't mind us!

DOCTOR: Is your father alive?

MISS AMELIE: No, he's dead!

DOCTOR: I see! Now I have gone so far that the only thing to do is continue. Herr Hall...

MISS THERESE: Our father was supervisor at the fire insurance company of Gothenburg.

DOCTOR: I see! Then I must beg your pardon! – Are you having fun in Paris?

MISS AMELIE: Lots! – Therese, did you see where I left my shawl? There's such a draught here. (*Stands.*)

MISS THERESE: You probably left it in the pavilion in the garden... (*Stands.*)

DOCTOR: (*Stands up.*) No, don't go out. Won't you allow me, I'll go and find it for you. – No, you sit still now! Just sit still! (*Goes out into the garden.*)

Scene 6

The MISSES HALL. FRU HALL comes in from the left fairly tipsy, with flushed cheeks and slurred speech.

MISS AMELIE: Look, there's Mummy! And in a state again! God, what is she doing here? – What are you doing here, Mummy?

FRU HALL: Quiet you two! I can be here just as well as you can!

MISS THERESE: Why have you been drinking again now? Imagine if someone comes?

FRU HALL: I haven't been drinking! What are you talking about!

MISS AMELIE: We shall be very upset if the doctor comes back and sees you. Come on, let's go in here, you can have a glass of water.

FRU HALL: That's a fine way to treat your mother, and telling me I'm drunk, your own mother!

MISS THERESE: Don't talk, just get in there! (*Leads her out, right.*)

FRU HALL: (*Reluctantly.*) What a way to treat your mother. Have you no respect for your mother?

MISS AMELIE: Not much. Now get a move on!

(*They go in to the right.*)

Scene 7

AXEL and CARL from the garden.

CARL: Well, you look perky, my dear Axel, and you have a more manly appearance than before.

AXEL: Yes, I have emancipated myself!

CARL: You should have done that at once like me.

AXEL: Like you?

CARL: Like me. I took at once my position as head of the family to which I found myself called on account of my superior intelligence and natural aptitude.

AXEL: What did your wife think of that?

CARL: Do you know I forgot to ask her! But to judge from appearances she found it quite fitting. Give them a real man and even women behave themselves!

AXEL: But power should be shared at least shouldn't it.

CARL: Power can't be shared! Either obey or command. Either you or me! I preferred me and she had to put up with it.

AXEL: Well, yes! – But she had money!

CARL: Not at all! She brought nothing more to the nest than a silver spoon. But she wanted a contract for that; and she got one. She was a woman of principle, you see! – But she's nice, she's very nice, you see, but then I'm nice to her too. It's fun being married I think. And then you see she makes such terribly good food!

Scene 8

As before. The MISSES HALL from the right.

AXEL: Allow me to introduce! Lieutenant Stark, the Misses Hall.

CARL: So nice to make your...– (*A look of recognition.*) – acquaintances.

(*The MISSES HALL are embarrassed; they curtsey and go out into the garden.*)

How did those women come to be here?

AXEL: What do you mean! They're friends of my wife, and it's the first time they're here. Do you know them?

CARL: Somewhat, yes!

AXEL: What are you trying to say?

CARL: Hmm! I met them in Saint Petersburg, one night!

AXEL: One night!

CARL: Yes!

AXEL: Surely you are mistaken!

CARL: No, no! It's no mistake. They were two very well-known young ladies in Saint Petersburg.

AXEL: And Bertha lets them into my house!

Scene 9

As before. BERTHA rushes in.

BERTHA: What's the meaning of this! Have you insulted those girls?

AXEL: No...but...

BERTHA: They came out crying and said they couldn't remain in those men's company! What has happened?

AXEL: Do you know these women?

BERTHA: They're my friends! That's enough isn't it?

AXEL: Not quite!

BERTHA: Not quite. Well, if...

Scene 10

As before. DOCTOR ÖSTERMARK comes in from the garden.

DOCTOR: What's all this about now? What have you done to those two little girls, who just ran off! I tried to help them on with their jackets, but they just pushed me away, with tears in their eyes.

CARL: I must ask: are they your friends Bertha?

BERTHA: Yes, they are! But if my protection isn't enough, then perhaps Doctor Östermark will take them under his, since he has a certain duty to do so.

CARL: There is some mistake here. Do you mean that I who have had connections with these ladies should be chivalrous towards them.

BERTHA: What kind of connections?

CARL: Temporary, the kind one has with such women!

BERTHA: Such women! You're lying!

CARL: I am not in the habit of lying!

DOCTOR: But I don't understand: what have I got to do with these ladies?

BERTHA: You preferred not to have anything to do with your children whom you deserted!

DOCTOR: They weren't my children. I don't understand this!

BERTHA: They were your two daughters with your ex-wife.

DOCTOR: Since you consider you have the right to be so impertinent as to make my family relations the subject of public inspection, then I shall answer you publicly! You seem already to have found out that I am not a widower, but rather divorced. Fine! Twenty years ago my marriage which was childless, was dissolved. Since then I have entered into a new relationship from which I have a child who was recently five years old. These two grown-up ladies are not, therefore, my children. So now you know!

BERTHA: But your wife threw you out...

DOCTOR: No, that's not true either. She walked off, or rather staggered if you like, and so she got half my income, right up until I found out that – – enough said. If you had any idea what it cost me in work and privation to support two households, then you would have spared me this unpleasant moment, but someone like you isn't going to take the time to think about it. You don't need to know any more, especially since this matter doesn't concern you!

BERTHA: I should like to know why your first wife left you!

DOCTOR: I shouldn't think you would like to know that she was nasty, small-minded, petty, and that I was too kind towards her! Imagine, you gentle-hearted, tactful Bertha, imagine if they really had been my daughters, these common friends of yours and Carl's; imagine how my old heart would have rejoiced to see again after eighteen years these children, whom I had borne in my arms through their nights of sickness. And imagine if she, my first love, with whom for me life first came alive, had accepted your invitation and arrived. What a rewarding final act to the melodrama you would have given us, what a noble revenge upon an innocent man.

Thank you my old friend, thank you for this repayment
of the friendship I have shown you.

BERTHA: Repayment! Yes, I know I owe you...your fee...

AXEL/CARL/DOCTOR: Oh! Oh!

BERTHA: I know, I know it full well!

AXEL/CARL/DOCTOR: No, for shame! For shame!

DOCTOR: No, I'm off! Horror! You're a charmer aren't
you! Excuse me Axel, but there's nothing I can do!

BERTHA: He's a fine man that one, allowing his wife to be
insulted!

AXEL: I don't interfere with your right either to insult or
be insulted! (*Music in the garden; guitar and Italian singing.*)
The singers have arrived, perhaps everyone would be
so good as to step outside to hear a little harmony after
all this!

Scene 11

*Everyone goes out into the garden. The DOCTOR is alone. The music
from the garden can be heard faintly in the room. The DOCTOR
walks around looking at the drawings on the right-hand wall over
towards the door to AXEL's room; FRU HALL comes out, walks
unsteadily into the room; stops and sits on a chair. The DOCTOR,
who doesn't recognise her, bows.*

FRU HALL: What's that music out there?

DOCTOR: It's some Italians, madam!

FRU HALL: I see; it must be the ones I heard in Monte
Carlo.

DOCTOR: Oh, there are perhaps other Italians!

FRU HALL: I do believe it's Östermark himself! – Yes,
there's no one so quick in his replies as he!

DOCTOR: (*Stares at her.*) Ah! – Imagine, that there are
things...which...are less terrible than the fear of them!
It's you Carolina! And this is the moment that for
eighteen years I have avoided, dreamt of, sought,
dreaded, desired; desired so I could feel the blow and so
have nothing more to fear afterwards! (*He takes out a
little bottle and wets his tongue with a few drops.*) Don't

worry, it's not poison; in such a small dose. It's for my heart you see!

FRU HALL: Oh, that heart. Oh yes! You always had such a lot of heart!

DOCTOR: It's strange that two old people cannot meet once in eighteen years without arguing.

FRU HALL: It was always you, who argued!

DOCTOR: All on my own? Eh! – Let's stop it shall we? – Let me try and look at you. (*Takes a chair and sits facing her.*) Without shaking!

FRU HALL: I've grown old!

DOCTOR: One does; one reads about it, hears about it, sees it, feels it oneself, but it's still terrible. I'm old too!

FRU HALL: And are you happy with your new – life?

DOCTOR: Quite honestly: it's humdrum; different, but rather similar.

FRU HALL: The old one was better perhaps?

DOCTOR: No, it wasn't better, because it was the same, but the question is if would have been better now, simply and only because it was the old one. One blossoms only once, and then one goes to seed; whatever comes afterwards is just chaff.

And you? how do you live?

FRU HALL: (*Offended.*) How do I live?

DOCTOR: Don't misunderstand me! Are you satisfied with – your life, I mean – why must it be so complicated talking to women. –

FRU HALL: Satisfied? Hmm!

DOCTOR: Yes, you were never satisfied! But when you're young, you want everything to be first-rate, and then you get third-rate, when you are old. Well! You said to Fru Alberg that your girls were my children!

FRU HALL: Did I! That's not true.

DOCTOR: Still lying! – Before, when I knew no better, I held you to blame for it; but now I know it's a fault of nature. You believe yourself in your lies, and you see, that's dangerous! But that's beside the point! Are you leaving, or would you rather that I went?

FRU HALL: I'll go! (*Falls back onto her chair and gropes around her.*)

DOCTOR: What! Drunk? – – – This is so unpleasant so dreadfully unpleasant, oh! For shame, I think I feel like crying! – Carolina! No, I can't bear it!

FRU HALL: I'm ill!

DOCTOR: Yes, you get ill, when you drink too much! Well! This is worse than I imagined. I have killed tiny unborn children to save the mother, and I've felt them quivering in the death struggle, I have sawn through living tissue and seen the marrow dripping like butter from healthy bones, but never has anything been so painful to me than the day you left. Then it was as if you went off with one of my lungs, and I could only gasp with the other! – Oh, I think I'm suffocating!

FRU HALL: Help me out of here! It's so noisy! And I don't know what we're doing here anyway. Give me your hand!

DOCTOR: (*Leads her to the upstage door.*) That time it was I begged for your hand; and it lay heavy upon me, that little hand. It struck me once, in the face, that fine white hand; and I kissed it nevertheless. – Oh! Now it's withered and strikes no more... Oh Sweet Naples! Joy of life, where have you gone? Left me like this woman! Who was once the love of my life!

FRU HALL: (*In the entrance hall.*) Where's my coat?

DOCTOR: (*Closes the door.*) In the hall presumably. – It's horrible! (*Lights a cigar.*) Oh Sweet Naples! I wonder if it really is so lovely in that cholera-ridden fishing port? *Blague*! probably! *Blague*! *Blague*! Women, love, Naples, the joy of life, antiquated, modern, liberal, conservative, ideal, real, natural, *blague, blague*!! All the way!

Scene 12

The DOCTOR. AXEL. ABEL. WILLMER. FRU STARK.

FRU STARK: Where are you off to Doctor?

DOCTOR: I'm sorry, it was just a little quid pro quo. Two strangers had sneaked their way in here, and had to be identified.

FRU STARK: The girls!

CARL: Yes, well that's nothing to do with you! I don't know; it feels like 'the enemy is amongst us'!

DOCTOR: Oh, you always see enemies, my dear Carl.

CARL: No, I don't see them, but I feel them!

FRU STARK: Well, come here to your friend then, and she'll defend you.

CARL: Oh, you're always so nice to me.

FRU STARK: Why wouldn't I be, when you mean so well towards me!

Scene 13

As before. The upstage doors open and two men carry in a picture. The MAID.

AXEL: What's this!

MAID: The concierge said that it was to be carried up to the studio, because he couldn't have it in his office.

AXEL: What is this nonsense. Take that picture away!

MAID: Madam sent for her picture herself.

BERTHA: That's not true! Besides it's not my picture. It's the master's! Put it there! (*The MAID and the men go out.*) Maybe it isn't yours, Axel? May we see!
(*AXEL stands before the painting.*)
Move aside a little so we can see!

AXEL: (*Moves aside.*) It's a mistake!

BERTHA: (*Screams.*) What! What is it! It's a mistake! What does this mean! It's my painting, but, it's Axel's number. Oh! (*She collapses.*)

Scene 14

As before. The DOCTOR and CARL carry BERTHA into her room on the left. The women follow.

ABEL: She's dying!

FRU STARK: God help us, what is going on! Poor little thing! Doctor Östermark, do something! Say something! And Axel standing there doing nothing.

(*AXEL and WILLMER are left alone.*)

AXEL: This is your doing!

WILLMER: Me?

AXEL: (*Takes him by the ear.*) You, but not all of it! You shall have your share. (*Leads him to the door, which he opens with one foot; kicks him out with the other.*) Out!

WILLMER: I'll get you back for this!

AXEL: I'll wait for that!

Scene 15

AXEL. DOCTOR ÖSTERMARK. CARL.

DOCTOR: What was all that with the painting?

AXEL: That was supposed to be sulphuric acid!

CARL: Tell us! Were you refused or her?

AXEL: I was refused on her painting! I wanted to help her, like a good friend, and so I changed the numbers.

DOCTOR: Well, this is a turn-up! She says you don't love her any more.

AXEL: She's right. That's how it is, and tomorrow we part.

DOCTOR: Part?

AXEL: Yes! There's no bond to break, it's untying by itself. This was no marriage, this was just cohabitation or something worse!

DOCTOR: The air's bad here! Come on, let's go!

AXEL: Yes, I want to get out – out of here.

(*They walk upstage.*)

Scene 16

As before. ABEL.

ABEL: What? Are the gentlemen leaving?

AXEL: Are you surprised?

ABEL: Can I speak to you!

AXEL: Speak!

ABEL: Won't you go in to Bertha?

AXEL: No!

ABEL: What have you done to her?

AXEL: I have conquered her!

ABEL: I can see that, her wrists were blue. Look at me! –
I never thought that of you. Well victor, gloat away!

AXEL: An uncertain victory, and besides one I didn't want!

ABEL: Are you sure about that? (*Leans towards him and
says quietly in his ear.*) Bertha loves you since – – – since
you conquered her.

AXEL: I know. But I don't love her any more.

ABEL: Won't you go in to her.

AXEL: No it's over. (*Takes the DOCTOR's arm.*) Come on!

ABEL: Shan't I say anything to Bertha?

AXEL: No! Yes! Tell her, that I hate and despise her!

ABEL: Farewell my friend!

AXEL: Farewell my enemy!

ABEL: Enemy?

AXEL: Perhaps you are my friend?

ABEL: I don't know! Both; neither! I am a hybrid...

AXEL: We all are since we are a cross between man and
woman! Maybe you have loved me in your own way,
since you wanted to separate Bertha and I.

ABEL: (*Rolls a cigarette.*) Loved! – I wonder what it would
be like to love someone? No, I can't love anyone; I must
be a cripple – – because I liked to see you two, until the
cripple's envy set me alight. – Maybe you loved me?

AXEL: No upon my honour! You were to me a nice friend,
who happened to be dressed as a woman; you never gave
the impression of being of another sex; and love, you
see, can and must only exist between individuals of
opposite sexes...

ABEL: Sexual love, yes!

AXEL: Is there any other?

ABEL: I don't know! – But it's certainly a shame for me!
And this hatred, this terrible hatred! Perhaps it would go,
if you weren't so afraid to love us, if you weren't so –
how shall I put it – moral, that's the word!

AXEL: Well then, you should all try to be in the name of
God a little more lovable, and not dress up, so that one
thinks of penal law, just looking at you!

ABEL: Do you think I'm so terrible then?

AXEL: Well look, you're going to have to excuse me! but you are dreadful!

Scene 17

As before. BERTHA.

BERTHA: (*To AXEL.*) Do you intend to leave?

AXEL: I did intend to just now, but now I'm staying!

BERTHA: (*Softly.*) What? You...

AXEL: I'm staying in my home!

BERTHA: In our...home!

AXEL: No mine! In my studio, with my furniture!

BERTHA: And me?

AXEL: You can do what you like, but you should know the risks! – You see, I have applied for a year's separation of bed and board. If you stay, which is to say, if you seek me out during this time, then you have the choice of prison or to be considered as my mistress! Do you want to stay?

BERTHA: Oh! – Is that the law?

AXEL: That is the law!

BERTHA: You're throwing me out then?

AXEL: No, the law is!

BERTHA: And you think I'm content with that?

AXEL: No I don't think you are, because you won't be content until I'm in my grave.

BERTHA: Axel! The way you talk! If you knew how I... love you!

AXEL: I don't find that unreasonable, but I don't love you any more!

BERTHA: (*Stands.*) Because you love her over there!

AXEL: No, of course I don't! I never have done, and never will do! What incredible conceit! As if there weren't other, more attractive women than you lot!

BERTHA: But she loves you!

AXEL: That *could* be true; I even believe she has implied as much herself, yes in fact I remember she actually said so; how did it go now?

BERTHA: (*Changes.*) You really are the rudest person, I have ever met!

AXEL: Yes, I should think I am!

BERTHA: (*Puts on her hat and coat.*) And now you intend to put me on the street? Are you serious?

AXEL: On the street, or wherever you like!

BERTHA: (*Enraged.*) Do you think, that a woman can allow herself to be treated in this way?

AXEL: You asked me once to forget you were a woman. Well, I've forgotten it!

BERTHA: But don't you know you have obligations towards the woman who has been your wife.

AXEL: To pay you mean, for good friendship? Eh? An income for life!

BERTHA: Yes!

AXEL: Here, have a month in advance! (*Puts some banknotes on the table.*)

BERTHA: (*Takes the money and counts it.*) You have some decency at least!

ABEL: Farewell, Bertha, now I'm going!

BERTHA: Wait a minute, so you're coming with me!

ABEL: No, now I'm not with you any more.

BERTHA: What? Why?

ABEL: No, I'm ashamed!

BERTHA: (*Surprised.*) Ashamed?

ABEL: Yes, I'm ashamed! Farewell! (*Goes.*)

BERTHA: I don't understand! – Farewell Axel! Thank you for this! Are we friends? (*Holds his hand.*)

AXEL: I'm not at any rate! – Let go of my hand, otherwise I shall think you are trying to seduce me again!
(*BERTHA goes towards the door.*)
(*With a sigh of relief.*) Nice friends! My God!

MAID: (*Comes in from the garden door.*) Mam'selle is waiting for you sir!

AXEL: I'm just coming!

BERTHA: Is that your new friend?

AXEL: No, she's no friend; she's my lover!

BERTHA: And wife to be!

AXEL: Perhaps! Because friends are for the café, but at home I want my wife! (*Moves as if to go.*) Excuse me!

BERTHA: Farewell then! Won't we meet again?

AXEL: Oh yes! – But in the café! Farewell!

The End.

CREDITORS

Fodringsägare

a tragi-comedy

(1889)

Characters

TEKLA

ADOLF[1]
her husband, a painter

GUSTAV
her previous husband, a lecturer
(travelling under an assumed name)

[1] Pronounced: 'ah-dolf'

A hotel lounge in a seaside resort. Door to a verandah upstage with view of a landscape. A table somewhat to the right with newspapers; chair left, chaise longue to the right of the table. Door to a room, right.

ADOLF and GUSTAV at the table on the right.

ADOLF: (*Kneading a waxen figure on a miniature modeling stand; he has his two crutches standing beside him.*) – – – and all this I have you to thank for!

GUSTAV: (*Smokes a cigar.*) Oh nonsense!

ADOLF: Quite certainly! For the first two days while my wife was away I lay powerless on a sofa just longing for her! It was as if she had gone off with my crutches, so that I couldn't budge. Then after I had slept for a few days, I came to life and began to gather myself together; my head, which laboured under a fever, set about calming down, old thoughts, which I had previously, popped up, the will to work and my creative drive returned – and my eye recovered its ability to see clear and true – and then you came!

GUSTAV: Granted you were wretched when I met you, and you were on crutches then, but that isn't to say that my presence has been the cause of your recuperation. You needed rest, and you had need of male company.

ADOLF: Yes, that's probably true, like everything you say; and I had male friends before, but when I married I found them superfluous, and I was content with the woman I had chosen. Then I moved into new circles, made many acquaintances, but my wife became jealous of them – she wanted me for herself, but the worst was, she even wanted my friends for herself – and so I was alone with my jealousy.

GUSTAV: You have quite a predisposition towards that particular sickness!

ADOLF: I was afraid I might lose her – and tried to forestall it, was that so strange? But I was never afraid she might be unfaithful to me –

GUSTAV: No, a married man never fears that!

ADOLF: No, isn't that remarkable! What I feared, was really that these friends would gain influence upon her and thereby indirectly power over me – and that I couldn't tolerate.

GUSTAV: You had different ideas then, you and your wife!

ADOLF: Since you have already heard so much, you can hear it all. – My wife has an independent nature – what are you smiling at?

GUSTAV: No, you go on! – She had an independent nature…

ADOLF: …Which meant she didn't want to receive anything from me…

GUSTAV: …Only from everyone else!

ADOLF: (*After a pause.*) Yes! – And it seemed as if she particularly hated my opinions, because they came from me and not because they were unreasonable. For often it might happen that she would come up with my ideas from previous dates and affecting them to be her own; yes, it might happen, that one of my friends would instil into her one of my ideas, and then she would like it. She liked everything, except what came from me.

GUSTAV: Which is to say, you are not really happy?

ADOLF: Oh yes, I'm happy! I have got the one I wanted, and I have never wished for anyone else.

GUSTAV: And never wanted to be free?

ADOLF: No, I couldn't say that I have. Well yes, sometimes I have imagined a certain repose, if I were to be free – but as soon as she leaves my side, I have longed for her, longed for her as if for my arms and legs! It's strange, but it seems to me sometimes as if she weren't anything herself but a part of me; an intestine that carries off my will, my lust for life; as if I have deposited with her the very knot of life, that anatomy speaks of!

GUSTAV: It may be so, when we come around to it!

ADOLF: How would that be? She is such an independent creature, with a mass of thoughts of her own; and when I met her, I was nothing, a child artist, whom she has developed!

GUSTAV: But then you trained her thinking and developed her, isn't that true?

ADOLF: No! She stopped growing and I carried on!

GUSTAV: Yes, it is strange, that her writing regressed after the first book, or at least got no better! But that time she had a fruitful subject – she is supposed to have executed a portrait of her husband – you never knew him? They say he was an idiot!

ADOLF: I never knew him, he was away for six months, but it does seem he was a prize idiot, to judge from her description!

(*Pause.*)

And you can rest assured, that her description was truthful!

GUSTAV: I am sure of it! – But why did she marry him?

ADOLF: Because she didn't know him; and it seems people never get to know each other until afterwards!

GUSTAV: Therefore one should never get married until – afterwards! – Well, he was a tyrant, of course!

ADOLF: Of course?

GUSTAV: All married men are – (*Tentatively.*) – Not least of all yourself!

ADOLF: Me! But I let my wife come and go as she pleases...

GUSTAV: That's the least you can do! Unless you think you should keep her locked in! But do you like her being out all night?

ADOLF: No, I certainly don't!

GUSTAV: You see! (*Changes.*) Quite honestly, it makes you seem ridiculous!

ADOLF: Ridiculous? Can one seem ridiculous for showing faith in one's wife?

GUSTAV: One certainly can; and you already are! Thoroughly!

ADOLF: (*Convulsed.*) Me! That was the last thing I wanted to be, we shall see about that!

GUSTAV: Gently now! You'll have another attack!

ADOLF: But why isn't she ridiculous, if I stay out all night?

GUSTAV: Why? That doesn't concern you, it just is so, and while you work out why, the disaster has already occurred!

ADOLF: What disaster?

GUSTAV: So anyway, her husband was a tyrant, and she had chosen him so that she could be free; because a girl can only be free by obtaining a chaperone, the so-called husband?

ADOLF: Naturally!

GUSTAV: And now you are the chaperone.

ADOLF: Me?

GUSTAV: Since you are her husband!

(*ADOLF distant.*)

Aren't I right?

ADOLF: (*Disturbed.*) I don't know! – You live together with a woman for years, and you never think about her, or the relationship, and then...you begin to reflect – and then it's started! – Gustav, you are my friend! You are the only male friend I've had! You've given me back the courage to live these past eight days; it is as if your magnetism has beamed into me; you have been to me like a watch-maker, who has repaired the movement in my head and pulled back the spring. Can't you hear yourself how I am thinking clearer, speaking more lucidly, and I think at least that my voice has regained its clang!

GUSTAV: Yes, I think so too; how can that have come about?

ADOLF: I don't know if it becomes a habit to speak quietly with women, but Tekla has always reproached me for shouting!

GUSTAV: And you lowered your tone and crept under the slipper!

ADOLF: Don't put it like that! (*Reflects.*) I think it's worse than that! But let's not talk about it now! – Where was I? – Oh yes, you came here, and you opened my eyes to the secrets of my art. I had it is true long felt a diminishing interest for painting, for it failed to offer me suitable material to express what I wanted, but when you gave me the reason for the phenomenon and explained why painting cannot be the right form for today's creative urge, then my eyes were opened and I realised that henceforward it would be impossible for me to produce anything more in oils.

GUSTAV: Are you quite sure now that you cannot paint any more, and you won't have a relapse?

ADOLF: Completely! – I've tried it! The evening after our conversation when I went to bed, I went through your argument point for point, and I felt you were right. But when I awoke after a good night's sleep and my head cleared, it struck me like a bolt of lightning that you could be mistaken; and I leapt up, took paint and brushes to paint, but it was all over! I had no illusion any more; it was just a mess of colours, and I was surprised that I could have deceived myself and others into thinking painted canvas was anything else than painted canvas. The gauze had fallen from my eyes, and it was just as impossible for me to paint again as to return to childhood!

GUSTAV: And then you realised that the real struggle of our time, its demand for reality, tangibility, could only find its form in sculpture, which gives body, extension in three dimensions...

ADOLF: (*Vague.*) Those three dimensions...yes, in a word – body!

GUSTAV: And so you became a sculptor; that is to say, you always were, but you became lost, and you just needed a guide to put you on the right path...Tell me: do you feel inspired now, when you work?

ADOLF: Now I live!

GUSTAV: May I see what you are doing?

ADOLF: A female form!

GUSTAV: Without a model? And so lifelike!

ADOLF: (*Listlessly.*) Yes, well it resembles someone! It's remarkable how that woman is there in my body, as I am in hers!

GUSTAV: The latter isn't remarkable – do you know what transfusion is?

ADOLF: Blood transfusion? Yes!

GUSTAV: You seem to have opened your veins too much; but when I see this picture, I understand a couple of things, which I have only suspected before. You have loved her terribly!

ADOLF: Yes, so much that I couldn't say if she was me or I was her; when she smiles, then I smile; when she cries, then I cry; and when she – can you imagine – gave birth – I felt the pains myself!

GUSTAV: Do you know what, my dear friend! It hurts me to say it, but you are exhibiting the first symptoms of the falling sickness!

ADOLF: (*Shaken.*) Me! How can you say that!

GUSTAV: Because I have seen the symptoms in a younger brother of mine who devoted himself to *excesser in venere.*

ADOLF: How, how did it manifest – itself?

(*GUSTAV vividly illustrative. ADOLF listens extremely attentively and involuntarily imitates GUSTAV's gestures.*)

GUSTAV: It was horrible to behold, and if you feel weak, I won't torment you with a description.

ADOLF: (*Angst-filled.*) No, go on, go on!

GUSTAV: Well! The boy had chanced to marry an innocent little girl with curly locks and dove eyes, a child's face and the pure soul of an angel. But she none the less managed to arrogate to herself the male prerogative...

ADOLF: What's that?

GUSTAV: The initiative, of course, and with the consequence that the angel was close to sending him to heaven. But first he had to mount the cross and feel the nails in his flesh. It was terrible!

ADOLF: (*Breathless.*) What happened then?

GUSTAV: (*Slowly.*) We could be sitting and talking, he and I – and after I had been talking for a while, he became white in the face, like chalk; his arms and legs stiffened and his thumbs twisted into his hands, like this!

(*A gesture; imitated by ADOLF.*)

Upon which his eyes grew bloodshot and he began chewing, like this!

(*He chews, imitated by ADOLF.*)

The saliva gurgled in his throat, his chest twisted as if it was on a carpenter's bench; his pupils flickered like a gas lamp, the froth was whipped up by his tongue and he sank – slowly – down – backwards – in the chair, as if he was drowning! Then...

ADOLF: (*In a whisper.*) Stop now!

GUSTAV: Then...Are you ill?

ADOLF: Yes!

GUSTAV: (*Stands to fetch a glass of water.*) There, drink this, we'll talk about something else!

ADOLF: (*Faint.*) Thanks! But go on!

GUSTAV: Well! When he awoke, he remembered nothing of what had happened; he had quite simply been unconscious! Have you ever been unconscious?

ADOLF: Yes, I have had fainting fits sometimes, but the doctor said it was anaemia.

GUSTAV: Yes, that's how it starts, you see! But believe me, it will be epilepsy, if you don't look after yourself.

ADOLF: What shall I do?

GUSTAV: You should observe complete celibacy for a start!

ADOLF: How long for?

GUSTAV: Six months at the very least.

ADOLF: I couldn't! It would ruin our married life!

GUSTAV: It's goodbye to you, then!

ADOLF: (*Places a sheet over the wax figure.*) I can't!

GUSTAV: Can't you save your own life! – But tell me, since you have so far taken me into your confidence, isn't there any other wound, some secret, that is tormenting you, because it's rare that there is only one cause of disharmony, life is so variegated and full of reasons for discord. Have you no skeleton in the cupboard you are hiding from! – You said just now for example, that you had a child that you sent away. Why don't you have it living with you?

ADOLF: It was my wife who wished it so!

GUSTAV: The reason? – Speak out!

ADOLF: Because, when it reached three years old, it began to resemble him, her ex-husband!

GUSTAV: Well! Have you seen her ex-husband?

ADOLF: No, never! I have just cast a fleeting glance at a bad portrait, but I couldn't see any likeness.

GUSTAV: Well, portraits never bear a resemblance, and he could have changed his appearance since then! – Meanwhile, this hasn't aroused any suspicions in you?

ADOLF: Not at all! The child was born one year after we were married and the man was out travelling, when I met Tekla here – it was right here at this resort – in this house furthermore, and that's why we come here every summer.

GUSTAV: So you couldn't therefore have any suspicions. And you don't need to have either, for a remarried widow's children often resemble the dead husband's children! It's infuriating, of course, but that's why they used to burn the widows in India, as you know! – Well, tell me! Haven't you ever been jealous of him, of his memory? Wouldn't it disgust you to meet him out walking and he with his eyes upon your Tekla's would say: 'we' instead of 'I'? – 'We'?

ADOLF: I can't deny that the thought has tormented me!

GUSTAV: There you are! – And you can never be free from it! You see, it causes disharmony in your life, that can never be resolved! Therefore you should stuff wax in your ears and work! Work, get older, and pile a mass of new impressions on the battened hatches, and keep that skeleton quiet.

ADOLF: Forgive me for interrupting! – But – it is remarkable how you resemble Tekla sometimes when you talk! You have a way of squinting with your right eye, as if you were taking aim, and your glance has the same power over me, as hers does sometimes.

GUSTAV: No, really!

ADOLF: And now you said that 'no, really?' with exactly the same indifferent tone of voice as she has. She also says: 'no really?', very often.

GUSTAV: Maybe we're distant relatives, since all people are related! It is strange though, and it will be interesting to make your wife's acquaintance and see that thing!

ADOLF: But can you imagine she never uses any of my expressions, but rather avoids my whole vocabulary, and I've never seen her use a gesture of mine. Generally, people tend to have marital likenesses, as they call it.

GUSTAV: Yes! But do you know what? – That woman has never loved you!

ADOLF: What!

GUSTAV: Well, I'm sorry! But you see, a woman's love consists of taking, receiving, and he from whom she will receive nothing, she loves not! She has never loved you!

ADOLF: Do you not think she can love more than once?

GUSTAV: No, one can only be fooled the once; then one's eyes are opened! You have never been fooled; and therefore you should beware those who have! They're dangerous!

ADOLF: Your words are like knives, and I feel as if something is being cut to pieces, but I can't prevent it; and it does good when it cuts, for there are boils that are bursting but would never break! – She has never loved me! – Why did she choose me, then?

GUSTAV: Think first about how she came to choose you, and if it was you who chose her, or she you!

ADOLF: God knows if I can answer that! – And quite how it happened! – It didn't happen overnight!

GUSTAV: Shall I try to guess how it came about?

ADOLF: You can't!

GUSTAV: Oh, with the knowledge you have given me of you and your wife, I can work out the course of events! Listen, and you'll hear. (*Dispassionately, almost jestingly.*) Her husband was away on a course and she was alone. At first she felt the charm of being free; then came emptiness, for I presume she was pretty empty after two weeks living alone. Then he comes along, and the vacuum is gradually filled. With comparison the absent one begins to pale, by the simple fact, of his being at a distance; – you know, the distance squared. – But when they feel their passions awaken, they become concerned for themselves, their consciences and for him. They seek protection behind fig-leaves, play brother and sister, and the more physical the feelings become, the more spiritual they cast their relationship!

ADOLF: Brother and sister? How do you know that?

GUSTAV: I guessed! Children play mummies and daddies, but when they get older, they play brother and sister – to hide what must be hidden! – And then they make vows of chastity – and play hide and seek – until they find each other in a dark corner, where they are sure no one sees them! (*With assumed sternness.*) But they sense there is *one* who sees them in the darkness – and they grow scared – and in their fright the figure of the absent one begins to haunt them – to assume dimensions – to be transformed, and he becomes a nightmare that disturbs their lovers' sleep, a creditor, knocking on the door, and they see his black hand between theirs, as they raise the cup to their lips, they hear his disagreeable tones in the silence of the night, otherwise disturbed only by the racing of pulses. He doesn't prevent them having each other, but he disturbs their happiness. And when they feel his invisible power to disturb their happiness, when they finally flee – but flee in vain from the memory, which pursues them, from the debt they've left behind them, and from opinion, which scares them, for they haven't the strength to bear the guilt, a scapegoat has to be dug up and slaughtered! They were freethinkers, but they didn't dare go before him and speak freely and say: 'we love each other!' – Well, they were cowardly, and therefore the tyrant had to be murdered! Is that right?

ADOLF: Yes! But you forgot, that she nurtured me, trained me to have new thoughts...

GUSTAV: I haven't forgotten it! But tell me, how come she couldn't train the other one too – to be a freethinker?

ADOLF: Because he was an idiot!

GUSTAV: It's true, he was an idiot! But that is a very vague notion, and in her novel his idiocy is described primarily, as being unable to understand her. Forgive me, but is your wife really so profound a thinker? I haven't found anything profound in her writing!

ADOLF: Me neither! – But I must confess, that I too have some difficulty understanding her. It is as if the mechanisms in our brains could never really engage with each other, as if something snapped in my head, when ever I tried to grasp her!

GUSTAV: Perhaps you are an idiot, too?

ADOLF: No, I don't *think* so! And I nearly always think, that she is wrong. – Would you like to read this letter, for example, that I received today. (*Takes a letter out of his wallet.*)

GUSTAV: (*Reads cursorily.*) Hm! That style seems familiar!

ADOLF: Masculine, almost?

GUSTAV: Yes, I have at least seen *one* man, who had a similar style! – She calls you 'brother'. Do you still play act with each other! – The fig leaf remains in place, although withered! – Do you use the familiar form with her?

ADOLF: No, I think you lose all respect that way!

GUSTAV: Really, is it to inspire respect in you that she calls herself 'sister'?

ADOLF: I want to respect her more than my own self, for her to be my better self!

GUSTAV: No, but be your better self yourself; perhaps it is more uncomfortable than allowing someone else to be! Do you wish to be beneath your wife then?

ADOLF: Yes, I do! I take pleasure from always being a little worse than her! So for example I have taught her to swim, and now I think it's fun to hear her boast that she is more skilful and daring than I. At first I pretended to be inferior and timid to give her courage, but in the end, one fine day, I became the inferior timid one. It seemed to me she really had taken my courage from me!

GUSTAV: Have you taught her anything else?

ADOLF: Yes – but it must remain between ourselves – I have taught her to spell, because she couldn't. But listen to this. When she took over the domestic correspondence, I stopped writing; and – can you believe it – now lack of practice over the years has made me forget my grammar here and there. But do you think she remembers that it was me who taught her from the beginning? No, I am the idiot, naturally!

GUSTAV: I see, so you are the idiot already!

ADOLF: In jest of course!

GUSTAV: Of course! But this is cannibalism! Do you know what that is? Well, the savages eat their enemies in order to absorb their outstanding qualities! – She has eaten your soul, this woman; your courage, your knowledge...

ADOLF: And my confidence! It was I who encouraged her to write her first book...

GUSTAV: (*Pulls a face.*) Aha?

ADOLF: It was I who gave her praise, even when I thought it was shabby. – It was I who drove her out into literary circles, where she sucked honey from the prize flowers; it was I who through my personal means kept the critics away from her; it was I who inflated her confidence with my own breath so that I became breathless myself! I gave, I gave, I gave – until I had nothing left myself! You know – I'm telling all now – you know, it strikes me now – and the mind is a wonderful thing – that when my artistic successes began to eclipse her – and her reputation – I tried to instil courage into her by making myself small and my art subordinate to hers. I talked so much about the insignificance of painting, talked so much and found so many justifications, that one fine day I became convinced myself of its insignificance; so that it was just a house of cards needing to be blown down!

GUSTAV: Forgive me if I remind you, that at the start of our conversation, you claimed she never takes anything from you.

ADOLF: Nowadays, yes! Because there isn't anything left to take.

GUSTAV: The snake is full and now it throws up!

ADOLF: Perhaps she has taken more from me, than I ever realised!

GUSTAV: Well, you can be sure of it. She took without you seeing, and you could call it stealing.

ADOLF: Perhaps she never did nurture me?

GUSTAV: Rather you nurtured her! Quite certainly. But it was her trick to make you think the opposite! May I ask in what way she nurtured you?

ADOLF: Well! To start with...hm!

GUSTAV: Well?

ADOLF: Well, I...

GUSTAV: No, it's her we're talking about!

ADOLF: Well, I couldn't really say now!

GUSTAV: You see!

ADOLF: Anyway...She had consumed my confidence too, and so I went into decline, until you came and gave me new faith.

GUSTAV: (*Smiles.*) In sculpture?

ADOLF: (*Uncertain.*) Yes!

GUSTAV: And you believe in it? In that abstract, obsolete art from man's childhood, you think that you can work with pure form – with the three dimensions, eh? – on today's scientific minds – that you can create illusion without colour, without colour, you say! Do you believe that?

ADOLF: (*Crushed.*) No!

GUSTAV: No, neither do I!

ADOLF: Why did you say you did then?

GUSTAV: I felt sorry for you!

ADOLF: Yes, so do I! Because now I am bankrupt! Finished! – And the worst of it is: I don't have her any more!

GUSTAV: What would you want her for!

ADOLF: Well, she was to be what God was, before I became an atheist; the object of my worshipping function...

GUSTAV: Bury your need to worship and let something else grow over it! A little healthy contempt, for example!

ADOLF: I cannot live without esteeming...

GUSTAV: Slave!

ADOLF: And a woman to esteem, to worship!

GUSTAV: The devil take it, you'd better bring God back! – since you needs must have something to cross yourself in front of! Some atheist, who's still superstitious about women! Some freethinker, who can't think freely about women! Do you know what the incomprehensible, the sphinx-like, the profound thing about your wife actually is? It's just stupidity! – Look here! She can't even spell properly! You see, there is a fault in the mechanism! The watch-case is that of a lever escapement watch, but the works are cylinder.

Just skirts; the whole lot of it! Put trousers on her and draw a moustache with charcoal under her nose; put your sober hat on and listen to her, then you'll see how different it sounds.

Just a phonograph, repeating your own – and others' –
words, ever so slightly attenuated!
Have you seen a naked woman? – Yes, naturally! A youth
with dugs on its chests, a man not fully developed, a
child, who shot up and then stopped growing, a chronic
anaemic, who has regular haemorrhaging thirteen times
a year! What can you do with them?

ADOLF: If it's all as you say, then how come I think we
are alike?

GUSTAV: Hallucination, the fascination of the skirt! Or –
perhaps because you have become alike. Levelling has
occurred; her capillarity has sucked the water level down
to her level! – Tell me something – (*Takes out his watch.*)
– we have talked now for six hours and your wife ought
to be here soon! Shouldn't we stop now, so you can rest?

ADOLF: No, don't leave me! I don't dare to be alone!

GUSTAV: Oh, just for a little while, and then your wife will
arrive!

ADOLF: Yes, she's coming! – How strange! I long for her,
but I am afraid of her! She caresses me, she is tender, but
there is something suffocating in her kisses, something
draining, deadening. And it is as if I were a child in the
circus, whose cheeks the clown pinches behind the
curtain so they will look rosy in front of the audience.

GUSTAV: My friend, it pains me to see you! I'm no doctor
but I can tell you anyway, that you are dying! One only
has to see your latest paintings to realise it!

ADOLF: Do you think so? But how?

GUSTAV: Your colour is water-blue, anaemic, thin, so that
the corpse-like yellow of the canvas shows through; it is
as if I can see your own hollow, putty-coloured cheeks
peeking through...

ADOLF: Stop, stop!

GUSTAV: Well, it's not just my particular opinion. Haven't
you read today's paper?

ADOLF: (*Starts.*) No!

GUSTAV: It's lying here on the table!

ADOLF: (*Reaches for newspaper without daring to take it.*)
Does it say that here?

GUSTAV: Read it! Or shall I?

ADOLF: No!

GUSTAV: I can go if you like!

ADOLF: No! no! no! – I don't know – I think I'm beginning to hate you but still I can't let you go! – You haul me up out of the hole in the ice, but no sooner am I up, than you beat me on the head and push me under again! While I had my secrets for myself, I had at least innards, but now I am empty. There is a painting by an Italian master, which shows torture; there's a saint, and they're drawing out his intestines on a capstan; the martyr is lying there watching himself get thinner and thinner and the roll on the capstan get thicker and thicker! – It seems to me now, that you grew while you hollowed me out, and when you go, you will leave with my entrails and leave behind a shell.

GUSTAV: Ah, how you fantasise! – Your wife is coming home moreover with your heart, I suppose?

ADOLF: No, not any more, since you have made a bonfire of her image for me! You have turned everything to ashes: my art, my love, my hope, my faith!

GUSTAV: It was already done!

ADOLF: Yes, but it could have been saved! Now it's too late, arsonist!

GUSTAV: We've just been burning the stubble! Now we can sow in the ashes!

ADOLF: I hate you; I curse you!

GUSTAV: These are good signs! You have some strength left! And now I shall pull you up again! Listen, now! Will you listen to me; and will you obey me?

ADOLF: Do what you want with me! I obey!

GUSTAV: (*Stands up.*) Look at me!

ADOLF: (*Looks at GUSTAV.*) You are looking at me again with those eyes, that draw me to you!

GUSTAV: And listen to me!

ADOLF: Yes, but talk about yourself! Don't talk about me any more; I am like a wound and I can't bear to be touched!

GUSTAV: No, there's nothing to say about me! I am a
teacher in dead languages and a widower, that's all! –
Take my hand now!

ADOLF: What terrible power you must have! It's like
touching an electricity generator.

GUSTAV: Know this then, that I was once as weak as you!
– Stand up!

ADOLF: (*Stands up; falls about GUSTAV's neck.*) I am like a
legless child and my brain lies open!

GUSTAV: Walk a bit across the floor!

ADOLF: I can't!

GUSTAV: You will do, otherwise I shall beat you!

ADOLF: (*Straightens.*) What did you say?

GUSTAV: I shall beat you! I said!

ADOLF: (*Leaps backwards, furious.*) You!

GUSTAV: You see! The blood has returned to your head
and your self-esteem has returned! Now I shall give you
the electricity. – Where is your wife?

ADOLF: Where is she?

GUSTAV: Yes!

ADOLF: She's – at – a meeting!

GUSTAV: Are you sure?

ADOLF: Absolutely!

GUSTAV: What kind of meeting?

ADOLF: A nursery school meeting![1]

GUSTAV: Did you part as friends?

ADOLF: (*Hesitantly.*) Not as friends!

GUSTAV: As enemies then! – What did you say, to annoy her?

ADOLF: You are terrible! I am afraid of you! How can you
know?

GUSTAV: I have three known factors, quite simply, and I
deduce the unknown! – What did you say to her?

ADOLF: I said – it was just two words, but they were
terrible, and I regret them, how I regret them!

GUSTAV: You shouldn't! – Tell me now!

ADOLF: I said: 'old flirt!'

GUSTAV: And then?

---

[1] Referring to a charity-run nursery for children of working-class
mothers with jobs.

ADOLF: I didn't say anything more!

GUSTAV: Oh, yes you did, but you have forgotten it, perhaps, because you don't dare remember it; you have stuffed it away in the secret drawer, but you shall just have to open it!

ADOLF: I don't remember!

GUSTAV: But I know! You said this: 'You should be ashamed to flirt, since you are so old that you couldn't get a lover!'

ADOLF: Did I say that! I must have! – But how can you know?

GUSTAV: I heard her tell the story on the steamboat, on my way here!

ADOLF: Tell whom?

GUSTAV: Four young men she had in her company! She falls for utter youths already, just like...

ADOLF: It's completely innocent!

GUSTAV: Like playing brother and sister, when you are mother and father!

ADOLF: You have seen her like that?

GUSTAV: Yes, I have! But you have never seen her, when you haven't seen her! I mean, when you haven't been present! And you see, that is the reason why a man *can* never know his wife! Do you have a portrait of her? (*ADOLF takes a portrait from his wallet; curious.*) You weren't there when it was taken?

ADOLF: No!

GUSTAV: Look at it! – Is it like the portrait you painted of her? – No! The features are the same, but the expression is different. But this you cannot see, for you insert your own picture of her! – Look at this now, as a painter, without thinking of the original! – What does this look like to you? I can see nothing other than an affectatious flirt, luring you into the game! See that cynical aspect about the mouth, that you never get to see; see how her eyes search out a man, that isn't you; see how the dress is low-cut, that her hair is rearranged, and her sleeves have worked their way up her arms! Do you see?

ADOLF: Yes – now I see.

GUSTAV: Beware, my boy!

ADOLF: Beware what?

GUSTAV: Her revenge! Remember that you have injured her in what constitutes for her the most unique and exalted place, when you said she couldn't attract a man! If you had said that what she writes is trash, then she would have laughed at your poor taste, but now – believe me, if she hasn't already taken revenge, then it's through no fault of her own!

ADOLF: I must know!

GUSTAV: Find out!

ADOLF: Find out!

GUSTAV: Have an eye to it; I shall help you, if you like!

ADOLF: Yes, since I shall die anyway – let it be, it's as well sooner as later! – What is to be done?

GUSTAV: Some information first! Hasn't your wife any vulnerable point?

ADOLF: Hardly! She has nine lives like a cat.

GUSTAV: So – the steamboat is blowing its whistle in the straits – she'll be here soon!

ADOLF: Then I must go down to meet her!

GUSTAV: No! You shall stay here! You shall be impolite! If she has a good conscience, you shall have a thick ear; if she is guilty, she will caress you!

ADOLF: Are you really sure of that?

GUSTAV: Not really, because the hare dodges and darts sometimes, but I shall track it down! I have my room here next door. (*Points to the door on the right behind the chair.*) I shall take up my post there and observe, while you play the part in here. And when you are done, we shall exchange roles; I shall go into the cage and work with the snake while you stand at the keyhole. Then we shall meet in the park and compare notes. But stand your ground! And if you become weak, I shall thump on the floor twice with a chair!

ADOLF: Agreed! – But don't go! I have to know that you are in the next room!

GUSTAV: I shall be. You can depend upon it – But don't be afraid, when later you see me carve up a human soul and

lay out the innards on the table here; they say it is
terrible for beginners, but once you've seen it you don't
regret it! – Just remember one thing! Not one word that
you have met me or that you have made anyone's
acquaintance in her absence! Not a word! Her weak point
I shall find myself! Quiet, she's already up and in her
room! – She's humming to herself! – Then she is furious!
– So, keep a straight back; and sit here on your chair, so
she has to sit on mine, and that way I can see you both at
the same time!

ADOLF: We have one hour left before dinner – there are no
new guests, the bell hasn't rung – we shall be alone for
dinner – unfortunately!

GUSTAV: Are you weak?

ADOLF: I am nothing! – Yes, yes I am afraid of what is to
come! But I cannot prevent it coming! The stone is
rolling, but it wasn't the last drop of water that set it
rolling, nor the first – it was all of it together!

GUSTAV: Then let it roll – there can be no peace before it
does! – Farewell for now! (*Goes.*)

(*ADOLF nods farewell; after standing with the photograph,
he rips it up and throws the pieces under the table; then he
sits on his chair, fiddles nervously with his cravat, puts his
hair in place, fingers his collar etc.*)

TEKLA: (*Comes in, goes straight up to him and kisses him,
amicable, candid, happy and charming.*) Good day to you,
little brother! And how are you?

ADOLF: (*Half conquered; resists, reluctantly jocular.*) What
wickedness have you been up to now, since you come
and kiss me?

TEKLA: Well, then I'll tell you! – I've been ruinous with
money!

ADOLF: Have you enjoyed yourself then?

TEKLA: Very much! But not at that nosh-up in any case! –
It was shit, as they say in Denmark! – But what has little
brother been up to, while Squirrelkins has been away!
(*Looks about her in the room as if she were looking for someone
or as if she had wind of something.*)

ADOLF: I have just been bored!

TEKLA: And had no company?

ADOLF: Quite alone!

TEKLA: (*Observes him; sits in the chaise longue.*) Who's been sitting here?

ADOLF: There? No one!

TEKLA: That's strange; the sofa is still warm and there's a dent in the spring from an elbow! Have you had a lady visitor?

ADOLF: Me? You don't think so!

TEKLA: But he's blushing! I think little brother is fibbing? – Come and tell Squirrelkins what you have on your conscience!
(*Pulls him towards her; he sinks down with his head on her knees.*)

ADOLF: (*Smiling.*) You are a she-devil, do you know that?

TEKLA: No, I am so ignorant of myself.

ADOLF: You never wonder over yourself!

TEKLA: (*She sniffs the air and observes.*) I think only about myself – I am a terrible egoist! – But, how philosophical you have become!

ADOLF: Put your hand on my brow!

TEKLA: (*Cooing.*) Have you got ants in your head again? Shall I chase them away, shall I! (*Kisses his forehead.*) There! Is it better now?

ADOLF: Yes it's better now!
(*Pause.*)

TEKLA: Well, now little brother must tell me what he has been up to? Have you painted anything?

ADOLF: No! I have stopped painting!

TEKLA: What? Have you stopped painting?

ADOLF: Yes, but don't scold me. I can't help it, if I can't paint any more!

TEKLA: What shall you do then?

ADOLF: I'm going to be a sculptor!

TEKLA: So many new ideas again!

ADOLF: Yes, only don't scold me! – Look at that figure over there!

TEKLA: (*Unveils the wax figure.*) Well look at that! – Who is it meant to be?

ADOLF: Guess!

TEKLA: (*Softly.*) Is it Squirrelkins? Isn't little brother ashamed!

ADOLF: Isn't it like you?

TEKLA: How should I know, when it doesn't have a face?

ADOLF: Yes, but there's so much else – that's beautiful!

TEKLA: (*Strikes him caressingly on the cheek.*) If he doesn't hold his tongue, I'll have to kiss him!

ADOLF: (*Fends her off.*) There now! – Someone might come!

TEKLA: What do I care about that! Aren't I allowed to kiss my own husband? Of course I am, it's my legal right.

ADOLF: Yes, but do you know what? The people here at the hotel don't think we're married, because we kiss so much! And that we argue sometimes doesn't dislodge their idea, because lovers are meant to do that as well!

TEKLA: Yes, but why should we argue anyway? Can't you always be nice like now! Tell me? Don't you want to be nice? Doesn't little brother want us to be happy?

ADOLF: Do I want us to be! But...

TEKLA: What's all this now again? Who's put it into your head that you shouldn't paint any more?

ADOLF: Who? You always sniff around after someone else behind me and my thoughts! You're jealous!

TEKLA: Yes, I am! I'm afraid someone is going to come and take you from me!

ADOLF: You're afraid of that, even though you know no woman can replace you, and that I couldn't live without you!

TEKLA: Yes, well it's not the women I am afraid of, it's your friends, that put ideas into your head!

ADOLF: (*Searchingly.*) So you are afraid – what are you afraid of?

TEKLA: (*Stands.*) Someone's been here! Who's been here?

ADOLF: Can't you bear me looking at you?

TEKLA: Not like that; you don't usually look at me like that!

ADOLF: How am I looking?

TEKLA: You are looking under my eyelids...

ADOLF: At you! Yes! I want to see what you look like behind them!

TEKLA: Go ahead and look! There's nothing to hide. – But
– you are also speaking in a different way – you have
expressions – (*Searchingly.*) – you are philosophising – aren't
you? (*Goes towards him threateningly.*) Who's been here?

ADOLF: No one except my doctor!

TEKLA: Your doctor! Who's that?

ADOLF: The doctor from Strömstad[1]!

TEKLA: What's his name?

ADOLF: Sjöberg[2]!

TEKLA: What did he say?

ADOLF: He said – well – he said amongst other things –
that I was close to getting epilepsy –

TEKLA: Amongst other things? What else did he say?

ADOLF: Well, he said a very sorry thing!

TEKLA: Tell me!

ADOLF: He says we weren't to live together as married for
a time!

TEKLA: There, you see! I thought so! Someone is trying to
separate us; I think I have noticed it for some time!

ADOLF: You can't have noticed it, since nothing has
happened.

TEKLA: Oh can't I have?

ADOLF: How should you be able to see what isn't there, if
it weren't fear which stirred up your imagination so that
you saw that which never existed. What do you fear?
That I should borrow another's eyes to see you as you
are, and not as you seem to me!

TEKLA: Control your imagination Adolf! It is the beast in
the soul of man.

ADOLF: Where did you learn that? From those youths on
the steamboat? Well?

TEKLA: (*Without losing her composure.*) Aha; well one can
learn something from youth as well!

ADOLF: I think you are starting to love youth already!

TEKLA: I always have; and that's why I love you! Do you
have any objections?

ADOLF: No; but I should rather it was only me!

[1] Pronounced: 'strehm-sta'

[2] Pronounced: 'sher-barrie' ('g' is soft in Swedish)

TEKLA: (*Joking, cooing.*) My heart is so big, you see, little brother, that it has room enough for many more than just you.

ADOLF: But little brother doesn't want any more brothers!

TEKLA: Come and let Squirrelkins pull your hair, for being so jealous, no, envious is the word!   .

(*Two thumps of the chair in GUSTAV's room can be heard.*)

ADOLF: No, I don't want to play! I want to talk seriously!

TEKLA: (*Cooing.*) Lord Jesus, he wants to talk seriously! It's terrifying how serious he has become. (*Takes his head and kisses him.*) Go on, give me a smile! – There, that's it!

ADOLF: (*Smiles reluctantly.*) Damn you; I swear you can do magic!

TEKLA: Yes, you see; and so you shouldn't fight with me, otherwise I shall magic you away!

ADOLF: (*Stands.*) Tekla! Sit in profile for me for a moment, so I can put the face on your statue.

TEKLA: Alright, why not! (*Turns her profile to him.*)

ADOLF: (*Stares at her; pretends to sculpt.*) Don't think of me now! Think of someone else!

TEKLA: I shall think of my latest conquest!

ADOLF: That youth?

TEKLA: Precisely! – He had such a sweet, sweet little moustache, and his cheek bones looked like peaches; they were so soft and pink, one wanted to bite them!

ADOLF: (*Darkens.*) Hold that expression on your mouth!

TEKLA: Which expression?

ADOLF: That cynical, insolent one, which I have never seen before!

TEKLA: (*Pulls a face.*) This one?

ADOLF: Exactly! (*Stands up.*) Do you know how Bret Harte[1] describes the adulteress?

TEKLA: No! I have never read Bret Chose[2]!

ADOLF: Well, the pallor which never blushes!

TEKLA: Never? But when she meets her lover, surely she blushes, even though her husband or Mister Bret never get to see it!

[1] Brett Harte: American author 1839-1902
[2] Tekla presumably means *chose* as in French for 'thing'

ADOLF: Are you sure of that?

TEKLA: (*In the same tone.*) Yes, if her husband can't send the blood to her head, then he never gets to see the charming spectacle!

ADOLF: (*Enraged.*) Tekla!

TEKLA: Little fool!

ADOLF: Tekla!

TEKLA: Call me Squirrelkins, and I'll blush nicely for you! Shall I, tell me?

ADOLF: (*Disarmed.*) I am so angry with you, you monster, that I should like to bite you –

TEKLA: (*Playfully.*) Come and bite me then! – Come! (*Stretches her arms out to him.*)

ADOLF: (*Holds her around the neck and kisses her.*) I shall bite you to death!

TEKLA: (*Playfully.*) Careful; someone might come.

ADOLF: What do I care about that! I don't care about anything in the whole world, so long as I have you!

TEKLA: And when you don't have me any more?

ADOLF: Then I shall die!

TEKLA: Yes, but you're not afraid of that because I am so old that no one would have me!

ADOLF: Tekla, you haven't forgotten my words! I take them back!

TEKLA: Can you explain how you can be so jealous and so sure of yourself at the same time?

ADOLF: No, I can't explain anything. But it is possible that the thought, that someone else has owned you, possibly rankles in my mind. Sometimes it seems to me as if our love is a fiction, a self-defence, a passion that has become a point of honour, and I know nothing that would torment me more than that *he* should know I am unhappy! Oh! I've never seen him, but just the thought that there is someone sitting waiting for my unhappiness, one who daily calls down curses upon me, and who will roar with laughter when I fall, just the thought of it is hounding me, drives me to you, fascinates me, cripples me!

TEKLA: Do you think I would give him that pleasure? Do you think I want to make his predictions come true?

ADOLF: No, I don't want to think so!

TEKLA: Can't you be at ease, then?

ADOLF: No, you torment me constantly with your flirting! Why do you play that game.

TEKLA: It's not a game. I want to be liked, that's all!

ADOLF: Yes, but only by men!

TEKLA: Naturally! Because, you know, a woman can never be liked by other women!

ADOLF: Listen! – Have you heard anything from – him, recently?

TEKLA: Not for six months!

ADOLF: Do you never think of him?

TEKLA: No! – Since the child died we have had no connections with one another.

ADOLF: And you haven't seen him, out and about?

TEKLA: No, he is apparently living on the west coast somewhere. But why are you worrying about that now?

ADOLF: I don't know. But these last days, when I have been alone, I have thought of him, how he must have felt, when he was left alone, that time!

TEKLA: I think you are having pangs of conscience!

ADOLF: Yes!

TEKLA: You feel like a thief, don't you?

ADOLF: Quite close!

TEKLA: That's nice! One steals women just as one steals children or chickens! – You regard me as his personal property or his real estate! Thank you very much!

ADOLF: No, I regard you as his wife! And that is more than property! It cannot be replaced!

TEKLA: Oh yes it can! If you were to hear that he was remarried, you'd get that idea out of your head! – You've replaced him for me!

ADOLF: Have I? – And did you ever love him?

TEKLA: Of course I did!

ADOLF: And then...

TEKLA: I got sick of him!

ADOLF: What if you got sick of me as well?

TEKLA: I won't!

ADOLF: If someone else came along, who had qualities which you look for in a man now, just imagine it! You would leave me!

TEKLA: No!

ADOLF: If he entrapped you? So that you couldn't leave him, so you would leave me, naturally!

TEKLA: No, not necessarily!

ADOLF: You couldn't very well love two at once?

TEKLA: Yes! I could, why not?

ADOLF: That I don't understand.

TEKLA: But things can exist, even though you don't understand them! Not everyone is made alike!

ADOLF: Now I am beginning to understand!

TEKLA: No, really!

ADOLF: No, really!

(*Pause, during which ADOLF can be seen trying with difficulty to remember something he cannot call to mind.*) Tekla! You know your frankness is beginning to be painful.

TEKLA: Even though for you it was the highest virtue, and one you taught me.

ADOLF: Yes, but it seems to me you are hiding behind this openness!

TEKLA: It's my new tactic, you see!

ADOLF: I don't know, but I think it's becoming unpleasant here. If you like, we can go home – this evening!

TEKLA: What kind of an idea is that! I have just arrived and I don't want to start travelling again!

ADOLF: Yes, but I do!

TEKLA: What do I care what you want! – You go!

ADOLF: I order you to leave with me on the next boat!

TEKLA: Order? What kind of talk is that?

ADOLF: Don't you know that you are my wife?

TEKLA: Don't you know that you are my husband?

ADOLF: Yes, there is a difference between the two!

TEKLA: I see, so you are taking that tone! – You have never loved me!

ADOLF: Haven't I?

TEKLA: No, because to love, is to give!

ADOLF: To love as a man, is to give; to love as a woman,
is to take! – And I have given to you, given, given!

TEKLA: Huh! What have you given?

ADOLF: Everything!

TEKLA: That's a lot! And if that is the case, then I have
received. Are you coming along now with the bill for
your presents? And if I have received, then I have
thereby shown that I love you! A woman only takes
presents from her lover!

ADOLF: Lover, yes! There you said a true word! I have
been your lover, never your husband!

TEKLA: Isn't that so much nicer, that, not to end up as the
chaperone! – But if you don't like that position, then you
are discharged, for it's not a husband I want!

ADOLF: No, I've noticed! Because, recently, when I saw
that you wanted to sneak away from me like a thief to
find your own circles, where you could strut about in my
feathers, sparkle with my jewels, I took the liberty of
reminding you of your debt. And I was transformed into
the nasty creditor, who you want to get away from; then
you wanted to strike out the promissory note, and so as
not to increase your indebtedness to me, you stopped
taking from my account, but went to others instead. I
became your husband without wanting to, and then came
your hate! But now I shall become your husband whether
you like it or not, since I cannot be your lover!

TEKLA: (*Smiling.*) Don't talk nonsense, little idiot!

ADOLF: Listen, it's dangerous to go about thinking
everyone else is an idiot except oneself.

TEKLA: Yes, but don't we all tend to think so!

ADOLF: And I am beginning to suspect that he – your
former husband – was possibly not an idiot.

TEKLA: Oh God, I think you're developing sympathy
for – him!

ADOLF: Yes, pretty well!

TEKLA: I see! – You'd like to make his acquaintance,
perhaps unburden your burgeoning heart to him! What a
pretty picture! – But even I am beginning to feel a

229

certain attraction towards him, since I have tired of
being a nursemaid, at least he was a man, even though he
had the fault of being mine!

ADOLF: You see! – But you shouldn't speak so loudly,
someone might hear us!

TEKLA: What would that matter, if they took us for a
married couple?

ADOLF: I see, you are developing a passion for manly men
too, and for youths at the same time!

TEKLA: My passions have no bounds as you see, and my
heart is open to all, to everything, great and small,
beautiful and ugly, young and old, I love the whole world!

ADOLF: Do you know what that means?

TEKLA: No, I know nothing! I just feel!

ADOLF: It means that your age is beginning to tell!

TEKLA: Are you at that again now! You'd better watch out!

ADOLF: You watch out!

TEKLA: What for!

ADOLF: For the knife!

TEKLA: (*Cooing.*) Little brother shouldn't play with such
dangerous things!

ADOLF: I'm not playing any more!

TEKLA: So, it's serious! Absolutely serious! Then I'll show
you – that you are mistaken! That is to say – you will
never see it, never know it, but the whole world shall
find out about it, except you! But you shall suspect it,
you shall sense it, and you shall never have a peaceful
moment again! You will get the feeling that you are
ridiculous, that you are betrayed, but you will never
have the proof in your hands, for a married man never
does! See how that feels!

ADOLF: You hate me?

TEKLA: No! I don't; and I don't think I will do either! But
that is possibly because you are a child!

ADOLF: Now, yes! But do you remember the time, when
the storm passed over us? You lay there like a baby
screaming; you came and sat on my knee, and I had to
kiss your eyes so you fell asleep. Then I was your nurse;
had to see to it that you didn't go out without combing

your hair, and send your boots to the cobblers, see that there was food in the oven. I had to sit by your side and hold your hand for hours, because you were afraid, afraid of the whole world, since you didn't possess a single friend and the simplest thing that was said would crush you. I had to talk courage into you, until my tongue dried and my head ached. I had to sit and imagine myself strong, force myself to believe in the future, and finally managed to get some life into you, when you lay for dead. Then you admired me; then I was the man, not that athlete whom you left, but the strong in spirit, the charismatic, that passed his vitality into your enervated muscles, charged your empty brain with new electricity. And then I restored you; provided you with friends, found for you a little court, which I fooled with the help of friendship into admiring you, set you above me and my house. Then I painted you in my most beautiful pictures, in pink and azure blue upon a ground of gold, and there was not one single exhibition where you weren't put up in the best position. Sometimes you were Saint Cecilia[1], sometimes Mary Stuart, Karin Månsdotter[2], Ebbe Brahe[3], and I created interest around you and subdued the braying mass into seeing you with my enchanted eyes, I tormented them with your personality, forced you upon them until you had won the all-compelling sympathy – and you could set forth on your own! When you were complete, then my strength was at an end and I collapsed from exhaustion – I had lifted you up and overstrained myself. I became ill, and my illness embarrassed you, now that life had at last begun to smile upon you – and I thought then that you were driven by a secret longing to get away from the creditor and witness!

[1] Patron saint of church music, martyred in Rome, saint's day 22 November

[2] Erik XIV's lover then wife. His unpopular marriage to her brought about his downfall, but she soothed his madness and they had children together even in prison. Pronounced: 'mawns-dotter'

[3] Childhood sweetheart of Gustav Adolf II (King of Sweden 1596-1674). Pronounced: 'ebb-eh brah-heh'

Your love began to have the character of the superior sister, and for want of anything better I grew used to it in the new role of little brother. Your tenderness remains, increases even, but it is fed with a grain of pity, which reserves a good deal of disdain, increasing to contempt, as my talent declines and your sun rises.

But at any rate, your well also appears to run dry, when I can no longer supply it, or rather, when you want to show that you don't want to draw from it. And so we sink the two of us! And now you want someone to blame! Someone new! For you are weak, and you can never bear a debt yourself, and so I became the scapegoat, to be butchered alive! And as you hacked away my sinews, you didn't reckon with maiming yourself, for the years had grafted us together as twins. You were a scion from my bush, but you wanted to cut away the shoot, before it had taken root, and so you couldn't grow on your own; the bush couldn't do without its main stem – therefore they both died!

TEKLA: By all of which you mean, you wrote all my books!

ADOLF: No, you want to say that to make me a liar! – I didn't express myself as crudely as you, and so I spoke for five minutes in order to give all the nuances, all the half tones, the transitions, but in your barrel-organ there is only one tone!

TEKLA: Yes-yes, but the summary of it all was that you wrote all my books.

ADOLF: No, there is no summary; you can't resolve a chord with one note; you can't translate a varied life into a single digit. I didn't say anything so blunt, as that I have written your books.

TEKLA: But that's what you meant?

ADOLF: (*Furious.*) No I didn't!

TEKLA: But the summation –

ADOLF: (*Wild.*) There is no summation when there is no addition, it is a quotient, one long, endless decimal fraction of a quotient when you divide and it doesn't come out even. I have not been adding!

TEKLA: No, but I can add up!

ADOLF: That I believe, but I haven't been!

TEKLA: But you wanted to!

ADOLF: (*Powerless, closes his eyes.*) No, no, no – don't speak to
me any more! It gives me convulsions! – Quiet! Get away
from me! You crush my brain with your crude pincers –
you put your claws into my thoughts and tear them apart!
(*Loses consciousness; stares ahead of him and twiddles his thumbs.*)

TEKLA: (*Tenderly.*) What's the matter? Are you ill? – Adolf!
(*ADOLF pushes her away.*)
Adolf!
(*ADOLF shakes his head.*)
Adolf!

ADOLF: Yes!

TEKLA: Do you admit that you were unfair just now?

ADOLF: Yes, yes, yes, yes, I admit it!

TEKLA: And do you beg my forgiveness?

ADOLF: Yes, yes, yes, I beg forgiveness! As long as you
don't talk to me!

TEKLA: Kiss my hand now!

ADOLF: (*Kisses her hand.*) I kiss your hand! As long as you
don't talk to me!

TEKLA: And now you must go out and take some fresh air
before dinner!

ADOLF: Yes, that's what I need! And then we can pack
and leave!

TEKLA: No!

ADOLF: (*Stands.*) Why? There must be a reason!

TEKLA: For the reason that I have promised to take part in
a soirée this evening!

ADOLF: I see, so that's it!

TEKLA: Yes, that's it! And I have promised to attend –

ADOLF: Promised! Maybe you said, you intended to be
there, and that doesn't prevent you from saying that you
don't intend to be there.

TEKLA: No, I'm not like you, I keep to my word!

ADOLF: Promises you can keep to, but you don't have to
keep to everything you say. Is there someone perhaps
has made you promise to go?

TEKLA: Yes!

ADOLF: Then you can ask to be freed from your promise, since your husband is ill!

TEKLA: No, I don't want to, and you are not so ill that you can't come along!

ADOLF: Why do you always want me to come with you? Do you feel calmer then?

TEKLA: I don't understand what you mean.

ADOLF: That's what you always say, when you know I mean something – that you don't like.

TEKLA: So! What is it now that I don't like?

ADOLF: Quiet, quiet, don't start again! – Farewell! And think what you are doing!

(*Goes out through the door upstage and then right. TEKLA alone; then GUSTAV comes in. GUSTAV goes directly to the table to take a newspaper, pretending not to see TEKLA.*)

TEKLA: (*Reacts; controls herself.*) Is it you?

GUSTAV: It is me! – I'm sorry...

TEKLA: How did you get here?

GUSTAV: I came by land; but – I won't stay, since...

TEKLA: No, stay! – Well, it's been a long time!

GUSTAV: It's been a long time!

TEKLA: You've changed a lot!

GUSTAV: And you are just as charming as ever! Almost more youthful! – But forgive me; I shan't embitter your happiness with my presence! And if I had known, that you were here, I would never have...

TEKLA: I beg you, if you don't find it indelicate, stay!

GUSTAV: For my own part there is no obstacle, but I imagine – well, whatever I say, I am bound to offend!

TEKLA: Sit for a while, you don't offend me, for you have the unusual ability – which you always had – of being delicate and tactful!

GUSTAV: You are too polite! But we can't presume – your husband would regard my qualities with the same indulgence as you!

TEKLA: On the contrary, he just now professed enormous sympathy with you!

GUSTAV: Oh! – Yes, well everything grows over, like the name you carve in a tree – and not even animosity can abide long in our hearts.

TEKLA: He has never felt any animosity towards you, since he has never seen you! – As far as I am concerned, I have always cherished the dream – of seeing you two meet for a moment as friends – or at least that you would happen to meet once in my presence – offer each other your hands – and part!

GUSTAV: It has also been my secret longing to see the one, whom I loved dearer than my own life – to see her in really good hands! And I have certainly heard much good of him, I know all his works, but would still have liked, before I grow old, to press his hand, look him in the eye and beg him to take care of the treasure, that providence has made his own. I wanted with that to quell the involuntary hatred that must be within me, and I wished to instil peace and humility within my heart, so that I may live out my sorry life!

TEKLA: You have spoken my own thoughts, and you have understood me! – Thank you!

GUSTAV: Ach, I am a lowly man and I was too insignificant to be able to put you in the shade! My monotonous life, the drudgery of my work, my narrow circles were not for your liberty-loving soul. I admit it! But you understand – you who have examined the human soul – what it has cost me to admit this to myself!

TEKLA: It's noble, it's mature to be able to own up to one's weaknesses – and it isn't everyone can manage it! (*Sighs.*) – But you were always of an honest, steadfast and reliable nature – which I valued – but...

GUSTAV: I wasn't – I wasn't then, but suffering purges us, grief ennobles us, and – I have suffered!

TEKLA: Poor Gustav! – Can you forgive me? Tell me, can you?

GUSTAV: Forgive? Forgive what? It is I who beg your forgiveness!

TEKLA: (*Turns.*) I think we are both crying – at our age!

GUSTAV: (*Changes tack carefully.*) At our age! Yes! I am aged! But you, you grow younger and younger! (*Sits stealthily on the chair to the left, upon which TEKLA occupies the chaise longue.*)

TEKLA: Do you think so?

GUSTAV: And you know so well how to dress!

TEKLA: It's you who taught me that! Do you remember how you discovered my colours?

GUSTAV: No!

TEKLA: Oh yes! Don't you remember – hm – I remember, that you were even angry on the days when I wasn't wearing something ponceau-coloured!

GUSTAV: I wasn't angry! I was never angry with you!

TEKLA: Oh yes, when you were teaching me how to think – do you remember? For I couldn't think at all!

GUSTAV: Of course you could think! Everyone can think! And now you're really sharp, at least when you write!

TEKLA: (*Unpleasantly affected, hurries the conversation along.*) Well, Gustav, it's been great fun to see you again, and in such peaceful circumstances.

GUSTAV: Well, I wasn't exactly quarrelsome was I, and you had quite a peaceful time with me!

TEKLA: Yes, rather too peaceful!

GUSTAV: So! But you see, I thought that was how you wanted me to be! At least that's what you seemed to say, when we were engaged.

TEKLA: Well, one doesn't know what one wants at that age! And then one's mother simply taught one how to please!

GUSTAV: Well, you've got a bit of action now! The artist's life I'm sure crackles with life, and your husband doesn't seem to be any kind of a slugabed!

TEKLA: You can get too much of a good thing too!

GUSTAV: (*Changes.*) What! I do believe you're still wearing the earrings I gave you!

TEKLA: (*Embarrassed.*) Yes, why wouldn't I? – We've never been enemies have we – and then I thought, that I should like to wear them as a sign – and a reminder – that we were not on bad terms – and besides, do you know what, you can't get these any more! (*Takes off an earring.*)

GUSTAV: Yes, that's all very well, but what does your husband say?

TEKLA: What do I care what he says!

GUSTAV: Don't you care! – But you do him ill by it! – You could make him seem foolish!

TEKLA: (*Short, as if to herself.*) He manages that so well by himself!

GUSTAV: (*Seeing that she has become fastened in the earring, rises.*) May I be of help?

TEKLA: Oh, thank you!

GUSTAV: (*Tweeks her ear.*) Your little ear! – Imagine if your husband saw us now!

TEKLA: Yes, then we should have weeping!

GUSTAV: Is he jealous?

TEKLA: Is he jealous! He certainly is, I can promise you! (*Thumping in the room on the right.*)

GUSTAV: Who is staying in that room?

TEKLA: I don't know! – So, tell me how you are, and what you've been doing!

GUSTAV: Tell me how you are! (*TEKLA troubled; lifts the sheet from the picture.*) Well! Who is that? Why, it's you!

TEKLA: I don't think so.

GUSTAV: But it's like you!

TEKLA: (*Cynical.*) Do you think so!

GUSTAV: It reminds me of the anecdote: 'How could Her Majesty see that?'[1]

TEKLA: (*Bursts out laughing.*) You're dreadful! – Do you know any new jokes?

GUSTAV: No, but you ought to.

TEKLA: I never hear anything funny any more!

GUSTAV: Is he a prude?

TEKLA: Oh yes! In conversation!

GUSTAV: Not otherwise?

TEKLA: He's so ill now!

[1] The title of a French farce that Strindburg had translated into Swedish: in it the Queen reports seeing some soldiers bathing naked, and is asked; 'How could Her Majesty see that?' (if they were naked, how could she tell they were soldiers?)

GUSTAV: Poor little fellow! But little brother shouldn't go nosing about in other people's bees' nests!

TEKLA: (*Laughs.*) You're dreadful!

GUSTAV: Do you remember the time when we were newly married – we stayed in this room! Eh! It had different furniture then! There was for example a bureau there by the pillar, and the bed was there.

TEKLA: Hush!

GUSTAV: Look at me!

TEKLA: Alright, why not!

(*They look at each other.*)

GUSTAV: Do you think one can forget something that has made such a strong impression!

TEKLA: No! And the power of memories is great! Youthful memories in particular.

GUSTAV: Do you remember when I first met you? You were a tiny, darling child; a little slate, upon which your parents and the governess had scrawled their marks, which I then had to erase. And then I wrote new things after my own mind, until you felt that you were a completed text. That is why, you see, I wouldn't like to be in your husband's position – well, that's his business! – but that is also why there is a certain pleasure in meeting you! Our thoughts coincide so well; and sitting here talking to you now, I feel as if I am opening bottles of old wine that I had bottled myself! I get my wine back, but it has been maturing! And now, as I stand on the point of remarrying, I have purposely chosen a young girl, whom I can form after my own mind, for, you see, a woman is a man's child, and if she isn't, he becomes hers, and then the world is upside down!

TEKLA: Are you remarrying?

GUSTAV: Yes! I shall tempt fate once again, only this time I shall put the horse into better harness, so that it doesn't bolt!

TEKLA: Is she beautiful?

GUSTAV: Yes, to me! But it may be that I am too old! And strangely enough – now that chance has thrown me in your path – I begin to doubt if it is possible to start that game over again.

TEKLA: What do you mean!

GUSTAV: I still have my roots, it seems, in your earth, and the old wounds are opening! You are a dangerous woman, Tekla!

TEKLA: We-ll! And my young husband says, I can't make any conquests any more!

GUSTAV: Which is to say: he has stopped loving you.

TEKLA: What he means by love, I cannot understand!

GUSTAV: You have played hide and seek for so long, that you can't get hold of each other! These things happen! You have had to play the virgin for yourself, so that he's lost his nerve! Yes, you see, it has its drawbacks changing partners. It has its drawbacks!

TEKLA: You reproach...

GUSTAV: Not at all! Whatever happens, happens with a certain necessity, because if it hadn't happened something else would have, but it did happen, and so it has happened!

TEKLA: You are such an educated man! And I've never met anyone I would rather exchange ideas with than you! You are so free from morals and preaching, you make such small demands upon people, that one feels free in your presence. Do you know I am jealous of your wife to be!

GUSTAV: And do you know I am jealous of your husband!

TEKLA: (*Stands.*) And now we shall part! For ever!

GUSTAV: Yes, we shall part! – But not without a goodbye! Am I right?

TEKLA: (*Troubled.*) No!

GUSTAV: (*Follows her across the room.*) Yes! – We shall take our leave of each other! We shall drown the memories in an intoxication that shall be so heavy, that when we awake, we shall have lost our memories – there are such intoxications you see! (*Puts his arm around her waist.*) You are dragged down by a sick spirit, who infects you with consumption! I shall breathe new life into you, I shall make your talent bloom in the autumn, like a remontant rose, I shall...

(Two women tourists can be seen in the doorway to the verandah; they look surprised; point their fingers, laugh, and move away.)

TEKLA: *(Pulls loose.)* Who was that?

GUSTAV: *(Indifferent.)* Holidaymakers!

TEKLA: Get away from me! I am afraid of you!

GUSTAV: Why?

TEKLA: You steal away my soul.

GUSTAV: And give you mine instead! You have no soul in any case, that's only an optical illusion!

TEKLA: You have a way of being impolite, so that one can't be angry with you!

GUSTAV: That's because you feel as if I have first claim upon you! – Tell me. When – and – where?

TEKLA: No! Poor Adolf. He still loves me, and I don't want to hurt him any more!

GUSTAV: He doesn't love you! Do you want proof?

TEKLA: How can you get proof?

GUSTAV: *(Picks up the pieces of the photograph from the floor.)* Here! See for yourself!

TEKLA: Oh! How shameful!

GUSTAV: There, see for yourself! – So: when? and where?

TEKLA: What a false wretch!

GUSTAV: When?

TEKLA: He's leaving tonight on the eight o'clock boat!

GUSTAV: So...

TEKLA: Nine o'clock!

(Noise from the room to the right.)

Who is staying in that room, making such a racket?

GUSTAV: *(Goes to the keyhole.)* We shall have a look! – There's a coffee table that's been knocked over and a broken water jug! Nothing else! Perhaps they've locked a dog up in there! – So, nine o'clock!

TEKLA: Agreed! It's his own fault! – Imagine what treachery, and from the one who preached honesty, and taught me to tell the truth! – But wait a minute now... how was it? – He was almost unfriendly when he greeted me – didn't come down to the pier – and then – and then he said

something about those young men on the boat, which I
pretended not to understand – but how could he know about
that? – Wait now – and then he started philosophising
about women – and you began to haunt him – and then
he said that he would become a sculptor because it was
today's art form – just as you predicted in the past!

GUSTAV: No, really!

TEKLA: No, really! – Ah! now I understand! Now I begin
to realise what a dreadful scoundrel you are! You have
been here tearing him to pieces! It was you sitting there
on the chaise longue; convinced him he had epilepsy;
told him he should be celibate; that he should prove
himself a man and revolt against his wife! Yes, it was
you! – How long have you been here?

GUSTAV: I have been here for eight days!

TEKLA: So it was you, whom I saw on the steamboat!

GUSTAV: It was I!

TEKLA: And now you thought that you would entrap me.

GUSTAV: I already have!

TEKLA: Not yet!

GUSTAV: Oh yes!

TEKLA: You crept up on my lamb, like a wolf! You came in
with your scurrilous plan to destroy my happiness, and
you set it to work until my eyes were opened and I
intercepted it!

GUSTAV: It's not quite exactly as you describe it! – This is
how it was in actual fact! – That it should go badly for
you two, was naturally my secret wish! But I was almost
certain that I would not have to intervene! And besides
I have had so much else to arrange that I really had no
time left for intrigues! But when I by chance was out for
a stroll, and by chance saw you with the young gentlemen
on the steamer, I thought the time had come to take a
look at you both!

I came here, and your lamb at once threw himself into
the arms of the wolf. I aroused his sympathy by means of
a kind of reflex, which I shall not be so impolite as to
attempt to explain; first I felt sympathy for him, since he

found himself in the same predicament I had once been in. But then he happened to pick at my old wound – the book, you know, and the idiot – and then I felt the urge to pull him to pieces – to mix up the pieces so that he couldn't be mended again – and I succeeded, thanks to your conscientious preparatory work! So that left you. You were the spring in the works and had to be wound up and broken. That set things humming!

When I came in to you, I didn't really know what I would say! I had I suppose several gambits like the chess player, but they depended on your moves, on how you played the game! One thing led to another, chance played its part and then I had you in the swamp. – And now you are stuck!

TEKLA: No!

GUSTAV: Oh yes, you are! – What you least wanted to happen has happened! The world – represented by two holidaymakers – whom I had not sent for – for I am no maker of intrigues – the world has seen how you have compromised yourself with your ex-husband and – filled with remorse crawled back into his faithful embrace! Will that do?

TEKLA: It ought to be enough for your revenge! – But tell me, you who are so enlightened, and right-thinking; how is it that you, who think that everything that happens does so out of necessity, and all actions are predetermined –

GUSTAV: (*Corrects her.*) To a certain degree predetermined.

TEKLA: It's the same thing!

GUSTAV: No!

TEKLA: – how is it, if you consider me to be innocent, since my nature and the circumstances drove me to act as I did, how could you think that you had a right to take revenge?

GUSTAV: Well, on the same grounds, on the grounds that my nature and the circumstances drove me to take revenge! So we're even! – But do you know why you two happened to draw the short straw in this struggle? (*TEKLA, contemptuous expression.*)

– why you allowed yourselves to be tricked? – Well, because I was stronger then you, and cleverer! It was you who was the idiot! – and him! So you see, you aren't an idiot just because you don't write novels or paint pictures! Remember that!

TEKLA: Are you completely devoid of feelings?

GUSTAV: Completely! – But, you see, that is why I can think, something of which you have very little experience, and act, something of which you have just had some experience!

TEKLA: And all this just because I wounded your self-esteem!

GUSTAV: It's no small thing! You should refrain from wounding someone's self-esteem! It's our most vulnerable point!

TEKLA: Vengeful wretch! Ugh!

GUSTAV: Wanton wretch! Ugh!

TEKLA: That's just my nature, isn't it?

GUSTAV: That's just my nature, isn't it? – One should find out about human nature in others, before one allows one's own nature free rein! You may get hurt otherwise, and then there will be wailing and a gnashing of teeth.

TEKLA: You can never forgive...

GUSTAV: Yes, I have forgiven you!

TEKLA: You have?

GUSTAV: Yes, of course! Have I lifted my hand against either of you in all these years? No! And now I came here just to take a look at you both, and you just cracked! Have I made any reproach, have I moralised or preached? No! I have had a bit of fun with your spouse, fit to make him burst!

But here I stand, being examined, while I'm the plaintiff! Tekla! Have you nothing to reproach yourself with?

TEKLA: Nothing at all! – Christians say that providence rules our actions, others call it fate, doesn't that make us innocent?

GUSTAV: Yes, to a certain degree, but there is a small margin and in there lies guilt in all its fullness; and the creditors present themselves sooner or later! Innocent but responsible! Innocent before God, who no longer exists; responsible before yourself and before your fellow man.

TEKLA: So you have come to make your demand!

GUSTAV: I have come to take back what you have stolen, not what you have been given! You stole my honour, and that I could only get back by taking yours! Was I right?

TEKLA: Honour! Hmm! And now you're satisfied!

GUSTAV: Now I am satisfied!

(*Rings for the PORTER.*)

TEKLA: And now you shall return to your fiancée!

GUSTAV: I have none! – And want none! I shan't be going home, for I have no home, and want none!

(*The PORTER enters.*)

Give me my bill; I am leaving on the eight o'clock boat!

(*The PORTER bows and leaves.*)

TEKLA: Without reconciliation?

GUSTAV: Reconciliation! You use so many words which have lost their meaning! Be reconciled? Shall we perhaps live together as a threesome? It's for you to bring reconciliation by making up for what you have done, but you can't! You have just taken, but what you have taken you have consumed and so you cannot return it! – Does it satisfy you that I say this; forgive me for you have scratched my heart to pieces; forgive me that you have dishonoured me; forgive me that I was for seven years a daily laughing-stock for my pupils; forgive me for giving you freedom from parental control, and releasing you from the tyranny of ignorance and superstition, for putting you in control of my house, for giving you position and friends, and making you into a woman from having been a child! Forgive me, as I forgive you! – I now release the bond! Go now and settle your account with the other one!

TEKLA: What have you done with him? I begin to suspect – something – terrible!

GUSTAV: Done with him? – Do you still love him?

TEKLA: Yes!

GUSTAV: But loved me just now! Is that true?

TEKLA: It's true!

GUSTAV: Do you know what that makes you?

TEKLA: You despise me?

GUSTAV: I feel sorry for you! It is a characteristic, I don't say a fault, but a characteristic, which is disadvantageous in its consequences. Poor Tekla! – I don't know – but I think I almost regret what I have done, even though I am innocent – like you! But maybe you can benefit by feeling what I felt that time! – Do you know where your husband is?

TEKLA: Now I think I know! – He is in your room here next door! And he has heard everything! And seen everything! And he who sees his own ghost dies![1]
(ADOLF is seen in the doorway to the verandah; pale as a corpse and with a streak of blood on one cheek, motionless, expressionless eyes and white froth about the mouth.)

GUSTAV: *(Recoils.)* Well, here he is! – Go and make up with him now, see if he will be as generous as me! – Farewell!
(Goes left but stops.)

TEKLA: *(Goes to ADOLF with outstretched arms.)* Adolf!
(ADOLF sinks down against the door.)
(Throwing herself upon his body and caressing him.) Adolf! My beloved child! Are you alive? Speak to me, speak! – Forgive your wicked Tekla! Forgive me! Forgive me! Forgive me. Little brother has to answer, do you hear! – No, God, he can't hear me! He's dead! Oh God in heaven, Oh my God, help us, help us!

GUSTAV: So, indeed she does love him! – Poor girl!

The End.

---

[1] Referring to the folkloric myth of the 'fylgia', a spirit presaging death

Strindberg: The Plays

Translated by Gregory Motton

Volume Two

The Chamber Plays
The Storm
The Burned Site
The Ghost Sonata
The Pelican
The Black Glove
The Great Highway
ISBN: 1 84002 086 5

Volume Three

The Dream Play
The Dance of Death I &II
Easter
Advent
Crimes and Crimes
Swan White
ISBN: 1 84002 089 X

Volume Four

The Bond
Before Death
The First Warning
Mother Love
Playing with Fire
To Damascus
ISBN: 1 84002 090 3